AF504329

Iron County, Missouri Marriages

BOOK "A"
BOOK "B"
NEWSPAPERS

James E. Bell

Iron County, Missouri Marriages

Book "A"
Book "B"
Newspapers

James E. Bell

PREFACE

Iron County was established in 1857 The county was formed
from parts of many counties, which included Dent, Madison,
St Francois, Washington, Wayne, and Reynolds Many marriages
are available from Washington, Madison and St Francois
Counties which are all pre-Iron County Most of the area that
Iron County acquired came from those three counties Iron
County has never lost it Court House since its emergence, so
much information may be found. It also has copies of almost
all the newspapers published in the county, especially the
Iron County Register which was its major paper for many
years
Book "A" and "B" in this publication are indexed separate An
index for Book "A" will start on page 43 and an index for
Book "B" will start on page 78. Book "C" and the marriages
from death notices taken from newspapers have no index as
only six pages are involved
It was never my intent to do a marriage book as that really
is not my "thing". So many times I needed marriages on
genealogy research, I had gone to the court house or library
and always collected additional marriages mostly because I
recognized the name Knowing my collection will only make a
huge bonfire when I breath my last, I decided to try and put
it in print Keep in mind the spelling of names as often the
same name may be spelled several different ways Some times
it was impossible to decipher the name. A lot of this was
read at the library on film making it even more difficult

Iron County Marriages
Book " A " 1857-1873

Date Of Marriage	Names	Minister
June 7, 1857	Rezen M Gunner -- Eliza Shepard	#119
Apr 1, 1857	Elijah Moss -- Dulcena Hampton	77
July 2, 1857	William O. Vance -- Martha Ann Inman	119
June 14, 1857	Oliver Hail -- Jane Parker	119
July 12, 1857	William Savage -- Adaline Shepard	119
May 21, 1857	Richard M. Rouse -- Elizabeth Huff	75
June 7, 1857	Harmon Bone -- Matilda Elizabeth Smith	75
Aug 6, 1857	Charles Collins -- Ann E Pease	103
July 22, 1857	Nathaniel Sutton -- Mary Vance	75
Aug 8, 1857	William J Hinchey-Lucinda Jane Holloman	103
Aug 13, 1857	William Imboden -- Margaret Shelton	44
Aug 9, 1857	Elias Kemp -- Dora Ingle	119
Aug 20, 1857	John Sutton -- Mary Ketcherside	21
Aug. 27, 1857	John G Imboden -- Mary E Petty	44
Aug 27, 1857	William L. Reyburn -- Elizabeth J Petty	44
Sept 3, 1857	Edwin H White -- Georgiana Mason	148
Sept 17, 1857	Tommy Joice ? --Rosana Smith	119
Sept 17, 1857	William Clark -- Eliza Parmer	119
Sept 24, 1857	Nathan Barthelow --Lucy Ann Fitzpatrick	103
Sept 24, 1857	Robert P Byrd -- Mary C Callaway	17
Aug 23, 1857	Pleasant I Norris -- Emly Stine	119
Aug 29, 1857	Joachim Seitz -- Maria Schwab	119
Aug 6 1857	Jacob Sutton -- Jane Pinkley	150
Oct. 8, 1857	Alexander Arthur -- Ann Shepard	104
Oct. 13, 1857	Frederick Ailer -- Eliza Roods	119
Aug 6 1857	Daniel Owen -- Catharine Kitcherside	75

Date	Names	Page
Sept 13, 1857	Isaiah Fulling -- Mary Ann Read	114
Oct 22, 1857	John Clapper -- Nancy Casteel ·	108
Aug. 30, 1857	Thomas Jackson -- Elizabeth Stubes	108
Sept 6, 1857	William Terrell -- Susan M Quisenberry	28
Oct 22, 1857	Joel Yancy -- Alice Q. Taylor	17
Oct 30, 1857	William Lewis -- Abigill Johnson	21
Dec 16, 1857	Peter Ake -- Caroline E Pease	103
Jan. 1, 1858	Antwine Beckley -- Teressa Spitsmiller	119
Dec. 3, 1858	Joseph Patterson -- Easter Jane Smith	119
Nov. 19, 1857	James M Logan -- Ann Stephens	94
Jan 3, 1858	William R. Gragg -- Elvira Gibson	143
Dec. 28, 1857	J J Lloyd -- Mahala Reed	48
Nov 30, 1857	John Coalston -- Martha Jane Horton	75
Oct 20, 1857	Israel C Crum -- Martha Ann Robinson	69
Dec 6. 1857	Jackson Brewer -- Elizabeth Morris	125
Dec. 14, 1857	Casus Rencau -- Angline Wiley	125
Dec 10. 1857	Johnathan Jorden -- Elizabeth Inman	106
Feb 4, 1858	Forest Meeker Newberry -- Mary Ann Blankenship	114
Jan 21, 1858	Barlow Harberson -- Sarah Bush	88
Jan 31 1858	James Chilton -- M S Johnson	88
Feb 19, 1858	John Tucker -- Martha Robinson	137
Mar 16. 1858	Harvy W Donoho -- Eleanora Mathews	131
Jan 12. 1858	Dewitt Bugg -- Mary Franks	145
Apr 11. 1858	George Warsing -- Susan Prough	6
Apr 11, 1858	Alfred Vickery Rouse -- Elizabeth Marinda Orrick	159
Mar 16, 1858	Henry Shrum -- Jane Row	88
Apr 27, 1858	Louis Seabert -- Caroline Richards	6

Iron County Marriages
Book " A " 1857-1873

Apr. 27, 1858   Charles Sahr -- Louisa Drachter   6

Apr 26, 1858   Thomas E Smith -- Widow Jane Reed   119

May 2, 1858   Harmon Bone -- Bethyer Rouse   101

May 2, 1858   Moses Baird --- Fanny Taylor   119

Apr 14, 1858   John T Young -- Sibirea Williams   97

Mar. 11, 1858   George F C Asher -- Martha Wezener   4

June 3, 1858   Issac W. Reed -- Mary M Messer   114

Apr   4, 1858   Harmon Bone -- Bethyer Rouse   101

Mar 8, 1858   William Rich -- Cidy Roe   108

June 18, 1858   Levi Ballard -- Elizabeth Adams   138

Mar. 4, 1858   Joseph Huff -- Rachael Eliza Smith   75

Feb 24, 1858   Cowans F Logan -- Martha E Carter   81

June 25. 1858   Joseph Mills -- Elizabeth Humole   125

July 15, 1858   John R Farrar -- Elizabeth Beal   6

Aug 1, 1858   Joseph M Reeves -- Sarah Jane Literal   6

June 6, 1858   Samuel H Bone -- Rodey E Pits   109

Aug 8, 1858   Ebeneizer Newton -- Nancy Jane Jones   153

Sept 2, 1858   Andrew J Henson -- Lucinda R Watson   150

Sept 21, 1858   John Coffray -- Mary Angeline Howard   29

Oct 3, 1858   Gotlieb Cocker -- Mina Haan   6

Oct 26, 1858   John Henry Zimmerman --- Emily Gaedart   6

Oct 10, 1858   James M Casteel -- Martha Lewis   150

Nov 2 1858   Nathaniel Richmon -- Martha Palmer   133

Sept 23, 1858   Thomas Exlexander Ketcherside -
                               Sarah Jane Renfro   75

Nov 21, 1858   William C Parmer -- Rhoda Smith   108

Sept. 30. 1858   Thomas Jefferson Reeves --
                               Sarah Jane Tullock   97

3

Iron County Marriages
Book " A " 1857-1873

Dec 5, 1858	Daniel S Miller -- Elizabeth A Brown	6
Nov 24, 1858	Simeon G Shular -- Susan A Sinclair	106
Nov 4, 1858	P S Sutton -- Nancy J Taylor	56
Nov 4, 1858	Henry H Jones -- Sary P Taylor	56
Aug 6. 1858	Benjamine Ammons -- Isabel Reed	125
Dec 12, 1858	William W Thompson -- Jane Chilton	125
Jan 15, 1858	William Hughes -- Eliza Ferrel	6
Jan 21, 1859	George J Tetley --Harriet Brill	6
Jan 20, 1859	William J McCollum -- Sarah Ann Swearengin	114
Feb 17, 1859	Eliga Baker -- Francois Juley Collins	29
Dec 5. 1858	John J Harbison -- Harriet A Day	30
Dec 26, 1858	William K Harbison -- Elizabeth Green	30
Feb 17, 1859	John McNeely -- Margret Emily Wiley	38
Jan 20, 1859	Hilery J Amott -- Narcicy Inman	106
Jan 13, 1859	Marion Jasper Orrick -- Elizabeth Malissa Edmonds	109
Feb 3. 1859	James T. Rose -- Lucrecia Carmack	125
Mar 17, 1859	John Shearer --- Elizabeth Hickman	125
Mar 10, 1859	Joseph Bruer -- Parallee Johnson	133
Oct 10 1858	Carrol R Peck -- Emily Lindsay	81
Mar 24 1859	Harlen L Mayo -- Eliza Watson	150
Mar. 31, 1859	John Collins -- Ann Sutton	150
Feb 28, 1859	John Emsly Browers -- Julia Ann Henson	157
Apr 17, 1859	William Swearengin -- ? ? McFadden	150
Apr 28, 1859	Frantz Dinger --Amalia Weise	6
Mar 27, 1859	Thomas Bell -- Susan Singleton	30
May 5 1859	Nicholas Brewer -- Rebecca Jane Casteel	133

May 24, 1859	Charles Sergert -- Louisa Feirbene	6
Mar 8, 1859	Elihu Farmer -- Margaret Ann Gragg	56
----------- [rec June 1, 1859]	Elisha Hardridge -- Elizabeth Thompson	88
June 2, 1859	Haver Zink -- Maria Gilbert	6
May 22, 1859	Alfred Goodman -- Margaret Loyd	125
May 22, 1859	Daniel Hubel -- Lousana Hoag	125
June 19, 1859	John M Smith -- Curneli Ann Lashley	34
Apr 24, 1859	Paul Harris -- Lurana Jane Edington	48
July 5, 1859	Robert S. Chauvin -- Martha Moore	46
Apr 21, 1859	Josiah Morgan -- Rhoda Harlan	110
July 17, 1859	David E Edington -- Nancy E Counts	138
July 17, 1859	Louis J Williams -- Martha Miller	138
May 26, 1859	Mathew A. Potter -- Catherine Kirk	157
May 29, 1859	D Alvasey Knapp -- Malinda Maberry	157
May 20, 1859	Robert J. Liles -- Mrs Malinda Brannum	110
May 20, 1859	James Oxyndine -- Eliza Jane Brannum	110
Aug 9, 1859	Charles B Snow -- Henrietta B Leonard	132
Aug 30, 1859	Richard F Trow -- Carrie L Peck	46
Aug 31, 1859	Andrew Buckner -- Elizabeth Calihan	138
Aug 12, 1859	William Shelton -- Marthy Catherin Sanders	85
Sept 15, 1859	Aaron Cheatwood -- Mary Baughman	133
Aug. 11, 1859	William Sutton -- Margaret Jane Vance	133
Sept 22, 1859	John Boss Jr. -- Mary Henry	46
Sept 29, 1859	John Henry Atchison--Martha Ann Parker	130
Oct 9, 1859	Henry Scholer --Caroline Sims	6
Aug 2, 1859	Thomas B Sandford -- Elizabeth Gregory	145

July 27, 1859	William H McMurtry -- Hannah J. Gragg	56
Oct 13, 1859	James Boggs -- Elizabeth Sherelds	29
Oct. 6, 1859	Dr N C Griffith -- Miss [Mrs] Frank H Smith [Frances Harriet]	46
Oct. 7, 1859	William Duregan --Generva Angeline Sensaboy	109
Oct 25, 1857	Charles Fooks -- Mary A Morgan	46
July 10, 1859	James C Polless -- Elizabeth Gray	89
Nov 3, 1859	Cunroy Meyer --Caroline Pershkey	6
Nov 3, 1857	John McMahan -- Mary Richardson	93
July 23, 1859	Elias Moore -- Sarah Elizabeth Mosses	82
Dec 1, 1859	Benjamine F Thompson --Caroline S Morgan	46
Sept 25, 1859	William Smith -- Martha Vianna Fortener	85
Nov 30 1859	Benjamine Funk -- Caroline Crowser	6
Oct 17 1859	Calvin Morman -- Annabela Legat	138
Nov 3, 1859	John Wilson -- Elizabeth J. Francis	48
Dec 8, 1859	William Allcorn -- Sarrah Jane Orrick	80
Nov 30, 1859	Charles Polk -- Sarah L Crist	58
Nov 6, 1859	Samuel Gore -- Mrs Sarah Mayberry	157
Jan 19, 1860	William H H Burk -- Amanda Rhyme	157
Dec 8, 1859	Robert Lane -- Elizabeth Jane Wilson	133
Jan 25, 1860	Daniel C. Horton -- Sarah Loyd	133
Jan 12, 1860	Allen Green -- Bebby Lewis	133
Feb 16, 1860	Samuel Warsing -- Delilah Prough	6
Feb. 5, 1860	Peter Shell -- Remitty Britenbaker	133
Feb 16, 1860	David Palmore -- Lucy J Petty	88
Nov 10, 1859	Dabner Imboden -- Elizabeth M Taylor	56
Feb 2?, 1860	Jacob i Ake Esqr -- Elizabeth Boswell	148

Iron County Marriages
Book " A " 1857-1873

Mar   1, 1860   William Casteel -- Martha Sutton   77

Mar   4, 1860   Hugh McLaferity -- Maloney C Pearson   138

Mar 16, 1860   William Resin -- Anna Landabaugh   6

Mar. 22, 1860   James Surridge -- Matilda Dennis   6

Apr   1, 1860   Giles Lee -- Mrs Elizabeth Seymore   148

Apr 22, 1860   Charles J Pooly -- Mary Jane Pierson   138

Apr. 22, 1860   Benjamine Vants -- Jane Brown   77

Mar   1, 1860   Daniel Jefferson Casteel --Nancy Canvas
                                                    Edmond   109

May 3, 1860   Simeon Frazier -- Tabitha Moore   46

May 6, 1860   Hiram Antis -- Sary Jane Robbs   77

May 6, 1860   James Smith -- Fanay Aldridge   77

May 6, 1860   James Reese -- Jane Sulivent   125

Feb 19, 1960   William Marlow -- Elizabeth Wallis   125

Mar   1, 1860   Joseph Sutton -- Malinda Inman   157

Feb 23, 1860   Joseph Leggett -- Mary Sutton   157

Mar   1, 1860   Issac Farmer -- Susan Stephens   56

Mar 15, 1860   John Laine -- Martha M Spier   102

Feb 23, 1860   John B Pratt -- Nancy Louisa Haynes   75

May 28, 1860   Charles Scherrenbeck -- Henrietta Lerke   74

May 8, 1860   David Park -- Malinda Huff   6

June 12, 1860   Thomas M Jones -- Nancy M Dugan   6

June 7, 1860   John Birch -- Miss N Smith   6

June 14, 1860   John S Marsh -- Isely Collins   150

June 21 1860   Harmone Bone -- Martha Aldridge   109

July 6, 1860   William L Tedder -- Frances L. Ramsey   4

July 10 1860   Archilaus Lee -- Mary H. Wood   10

Apr 5, 1860	William Rutledge -- Mary Imboden	17
July 28, 1860	Frederick Wessenstein -- Mary Faught	6
Aug 2 1860	James Alex Midleton -- Elizabeth Hall	6
Aug 12, 1860	James Parsons -- Nancy Eliz Leadbetter	6
Aug 16 1860	James McMain -- Elizabeth Renicks	108
May 29 1860	James Willis -- Mary E Hood	116
July 12, 1860	Jesse Willis -- Martha Jane Compton	116
June 3, 1860	Abraham Howard -- Martha Ann Davidson	116
Aug 12, 1860	William H Ghrist--Mary E Vickers	116
July 5, 1860	Jonathan Milburn -- Jane Sutton	147
June 29, 1860	Camel Johnston -- Charolotte Hannah	133
Sept 30, 1860	Elijah McFerson -- Mary Jane Chaplin	98
Aug 16, 1860	James M Amett -- Lenora Palmer	48
Oct 23, 1860	Wm T McClanahan -- Mary Lusinda McDowell	64
Aug 20, 1860	Anthony Savage -- Elizabeth Berlanda Boothe	109
Oct 10, 1860	John Stewart -- Mrs Nancy Brewer	95
Aug 12 1860	Evans S. Fuller -- Mary Ferrel	157
Aug 26, 1060	Robert Maberry -- Jane Henson	157
Sept 5, 1860	Jesse Roe -- Mary Jane Morton	109
Aug 30, 1860	Charles K Henderson -- Cyntha Strickland	123
Sept 21, 1860	J C Spencer -- C J Carpenter	6
Nov 15 1860	Frederic J Tetley -- Elizabeth J Bland	46
Sept 13, 1860	William Strickland -- Telitha Davis	30
Oct 13, 1860	William Beck -- Fredericke Brand	45
Dec 20 1860	William Buford -- Irene Guliver	17
Nov 22 1860	Issac C Harris -- Mary Elizabeth Ringer	17

Iron County Marriages
Book " A " 1857-1873

Nov   22, 1860   Charles H Taylor -- Mary Eliz Highley   29

Nov   22, 1860   T L Steward -- Mary Ann Brooks   85

Feb   3, 1861   James Cenceboy -- Louisa Odom   89

Dec   20, 1860   Frederick Willford--Conradina Fasterling 45

Feb   26 1860   Ferguus Sloan -- Elizabeth Thomas   134

Dec   25, 1860   Joseph Eckels Muffley - Mary Jane Logan 134

Feb   26. 1861   Robert A Callison -- Nancy J Casteel   157

Oct   21, 1860   John Carnahan -- ---- Dickson   156

Jan   31, 1861   James M Cole -- Sarah S Palmer   48

Dec   15, 1860   David Messer -- Mary Ann McCalister   138

Mar   18, 1861   Park H Peter -- Hattie Hall   46

Apr   1, 1861   Andrew Woerner -- Elizabetha Lammsback   74

Mar   21, 1861   Carl Heinricks -- Caroline Westeney   45

Apr   4, 1861   James W McNeely -- Nancy Jane Brewer   95
                  { groom age 23, bride age 23 }

Apr   25 1861   Adolph Dettmer -- Eliza Arnold   14

Mar   14, 1861   James Morton -- Rebecca Edmonds   109

Mar   21, 1861   Robert Gragg -- Mary Westerman   5

Feb   13, 1860   Samuel Quisenberry -- Isabella Webb   56

June 16, 1861   Karl Van Rothen -- Elizabeth Boss   45

June 16 1861   Aaron Livingstone -- Catherne Sowers   45

Apr   4 1860   Ezekiel Inman -- Amanda Watson   157

Apr   14 1861   Samuel Smith -- Emily Hartgrove   136

Mar   28, 1861   James J Neely -- Mary M Imboden   143

Sept 10. 1861   E P Child -- Lucie H Mitchell   46

July 14. 1861   Abarham Dean -- Elizabeth Underwood   157

Dec   1. 1861   Frank Ernst -- Mrs Jane M Miller   46

9

Dec 3, 1861   J Edmiston -- Elmy Frame   45

Aug 18, 1861   William Crocker Sr -- Martha Thompson   85

July 25, 1861   Benjamine F Brooks --Elizabeth Thompson 85

Aug. 8, 1861   William Crocker Jr. -- Marinda Thompson   85

Dec. 24, 1861   Robert Dines -- Sarah J B Smith   46

Dec 24, 1861   William H Hill -- Samira J Martin   159

Dec 29, 1861   Finley Adams -- Martha Cole   45

Jan 17, 1862   Elias Gibson -- Elizabeth Thurman   45

Jan 23, 1862   James Forgerson -- Mrs Penelope Caroline
                                                Green   46

Dec 13, 1861   Samuel Tullock -- Eliza Green   77

Dec 25, 1861   Oran Fuller -- Elvira Arnett   77

Jan 23, 1862   William W Dyer -- Elizabeth Green   46

Jan 4, 1862   John Denby -- Maty Boswell   159

Mar 18 1862   David Young -- Rebecca Hall   46

Mar 2 1862   Thomas Vanburen Boren --Martha Jane Smith 4

May 25, 1862   William E Burns -- Martha J Brown   46

Mar 20, 1862   Samuel Imboden -- Mary E Warner   17

Apr 1, 1862   Issac Nichols -- Eliza Hickman   125

Oct 19, 1861   John Crowley -- Irena Miller   102

Dec 8, 1861   Bluford W Rose -- Elizabeth Jackson   102

Apr 7 1862   James Hartridge -- Sarah Ratliff   102

June 1, 1862   George B Cole -- Cornelia Dryan   143

June 26, 1862   James Wilson -- Lucinda Ellen Brock   66

Oct 8, 1845   James M Johnson -- Lucinda Jane Shearer
[By S C Murray J P Marriage verified by John W Carmichal
Clerk of cc of Massac Co Il Rec Iron Co Aug 2, 1862]

July 20 1862   Peter Hanger Louis --Mary Loucinda Clay 140

July 20, 1862   George Vickmarm -- Elizabeth Kolb   16

Iron County Marriages
Book " A " 1857-1873

Oct   1, 1862   William Parman -- Eliza Jane Brock   66

Oct   27, 1862   James Turner -- Mary J Symps   107

Oct. 9, 1862   George W Crossgrove -- Eliza Casteel   46

Nov. 23, 1862   Isaac M Johnson -- Susan I Thomas   46

Nov   25, 1862   F Zuber -- Mrs M I Howlet   46

Oct   29, 1862   Ferdenand Schmitz -- Katharina Kolb   66

Dec. 6 1862   Hugh Hunter -- Anna M Groves   46

Jan   14, 1863   William M Pence -- Jane Legbetter   46

Nov   16, 1862   George W Stephens -- Elizabeth Smith   56

Sept 21, 1862   Oscar Rupe -- Milissa Webb   56

Nov   16, 1862   Jacob Ivester -- Mary Jane Carnahan ?   48

Jan   29, 1863   Ezra C. Tual -- Virena M Evans   17

Feb   5, 1863   Louis Labrash -- Catherine Hoy   62

Feb. 20, 1863   Joshua B Brown -- Catherine Shafer   62

Feb   12, 1863   George W Swaringen -- Mary Smith   77

Feb   12 1863   William S Reed -- Mary S Robbs   77

Feb   1, 1863   John Frett -- Catherine S Whittmore   62

Feb   15, 1863   John Linz -- Auguste Engleman   45

Feb   8, 1863   William Custead -- Lydia Harman   24

Mar   4, 1863   William Griffith -- Mary A McAlister   46

Jan   8, 1863   William F Edwards -- Sarah E Jones   49

Feb. 12, 1863   Samuel Black -- Mary Jane Bell   88

Mar   20, 1863   John Britton -- Nancy Ann Hall   45

Mar   3, 1863   William Hollats -- Auguste Funk   45

Jan. 4, 1863   Robert Thomason -- Ellener Hews   117

Apr   7, 1863   Henry Dusenberry -- Martha Jane Adams   46

Apr   2, 1863   Moses Menger -- Nancy Site   88

Apr 8, 1863   Andrew Jackson Wilson -- Mary Jane
                                          Davidson   24

Apr 7, 1863   Jacob Grandhomme -- Amanda Laura Weise   45

Apr 26, 1863   O S Ezell -- Clarissa Jane Bushan   7

Mar 26, 1863   Elis Carter -- Julia Manerva Thacker   138

Apr 16, 1863   Henry Whit -- Sarah Angeline Young   59

May 3, 1863   Frederick Granky -- Peggy Ann Wright   62

May 4, 1863   Charles Roeslein -- Henrietta Hollatz   45

Feb 26, 1863   Lindsey Ashberry -- Matilda Absher   77

Apr 5, 1863   James Smith -- Elizabeth Lackey   77

May 25, 1863   George B Tobin -- Mrs Nancy Fitzwater   24

May 21, 1863   William P Adair -- Mrs Elizabeth W
                                           Bosworth 46

Mar 10, 1863   Pierre R Ridgely -- Julia A Thomas   81

May 30, 1863   Josiah Bradshaw -- Mrs Margaret McKinney 86

May 30, 1863   Lewis Bales -- Sarah Agier   86

May 28, 1863   V B Shouf -- Clarie Hurst   62

June 5, 1863   Stephen D Edgar -- Martha J Adams   24

June 22, 1863   John W Honey -- Harriet Beck   62

Mar 30, 1863   Isiah E Sherrill-Mrs Permelia Stegall 158

June 28, 1863   Michael Caserly -- Mary Gibson   24

July 16, 1863   William Alexander Mires --
                                  Frances Catherine Slone 88

Aug 2, 1863   Henry Boss -- Lina Behrns   45

July 4 1863   James Brumphield Carder --
                                    Sarah Elizabeth Head 140

May 21, 1863   Alexander Alley -- Anney Livingston   7

Aug 6 1863   Samuel Jefferson Robbins --
                                  Angeline Rebecca Baker   17

Iron County Marriages
Book " A " 1857-1873

Aug 2, 1863	Issac T Reeder -- Sarah Ann Reed	77
Aug 16, 1863	William Lafayett Crain -- Emiley Armenta Robertson	77
Aug. 4, 1863	Riley Bowlin -- Julian T Posten	48
Aug 6, 1860	James L Brooks -- Louisa Bell	88
Sept 1, 1863	Stephen T Dunklin -- Sarah A Watts	17
Aug. 9, 1863	Samuel Howard -- Cynthya Ann Ross	125
Sept 13, 1863	Henry Schaefer -- Wilhelmina Grill	45
Oct 1, 1863	Thomas T Cook -- Nancy Jane Ellis	17
Oct 4, 1863	James McGregor -- Jane Ragan	24
Nov. 1, 1863	John W. Speck --Margaret E Stevens	17
Nov 2, 1861	Christian Millsap -- Catherine S Boci	45
Oct 4, 1863	John Reed -- Mrs Ann M Dean	80
June 22, 1863	John Sumpter -- Margaret Trollinger	4
Sept 13, 1863	Elijah Barrec -- Sarah Blanton	75
Sept 13 1863	George W Pinkley -- Mary M Smith	75
Oct 28, 1863	Andy S Love -- Elizabeth C Rayfield	75
Mar 12, 1863	Daniel Horton Jr -- Mrs Jane Haunapple	102
Nov 12, 1863	Jerome Nearren -- Launey Ramsey	88
Oct 1, 1863	John F Ramsey -- Elizabeth Cotrell	88
Jan 13, 1863	George Sloan -- Catherine Henderson	56
Nov 10 1863	Adison Inman -- Mrs Viena McDowel	77
Dec 5, 1863	Benjamine Hohanstricet -- Matilda Salsberry	24
Dec 6, 1863	A B Cowan -- Sarah Moody	24
Sept 23 1863	Jonathan C Tournbaugh -- Mary Ann Williams	158
Dec 17, 1863	William Brouner -- Mrs Lizzie Oden	24
Nov 5, 1863	William J Fuget -- Frances Reaves	17

Iron County Marriages
Book " A " 1857-1873

Dec	10	1863	John Smith -- Maria R Brown	17

Dec   10   1863   John Smith -- Maria R Brown   17

Jan   21, 1864   Stephen Ballew -- Emiley Joiner   24

Nov   25, 1863   James Mills -- Elen Reven   102

Jan   28, 1864   Joseph Piece -- Rosa O'Donnell   46

Jan. 7, 1864   Cimeon Crisco -- Manervia Shrum   88

Feb   16, 1864   John N Berryman -- Ann Reyburn   17

Feb   20, 1864   William C Houston -- Elizabeth Daniels   45

Feb   29, 1863   William Shaffner -- Maria Frissell   45

Mar   6. 1864   Eugene Van Erden --- Lizzie Kearney   45

Dec   31, 1863   James Stacy Bell -- Lucinda Trolinger   110

Mar   20. 1864   Richard M Sumpter -- Martha Elizabeth
                                                    Hicks 45

Jan   23, 1864   James Turner -- Elizabeth Perigan   7

Apr   5, 1864   Louis Kaesenhagen -- Elizza Keffer   45

Apr   6. 1864   Augustus Ginter -- Mary Vaughn   24

Apr   17 1864   George Reid -- Mrs Sarah Epler   45

Apr   17, 1864   H M Wood -- Mrs Sarah Joiner   45

Apr   25, 1864   Henry Sladeck -- Louisa Margaretha----?   45

Apr   28. 1864   Elihu Dunn -- Margaret E Pinkley   150

May   1, 1864   Frederick Oehler -- Maria Richter   57

Mar   11, 1864   Andrew Eaden -- Nancy Jane Love   77

Mar   7 1864   James H Bell -- Elizabeth Goggin   110

Oct   28, 1864   William H Anderson -- Elizabeth
                                      Catherine Woods 23

May   8, 1864   William Sharp -- Sarah Baxter   150

Mar   27 1864   Jesse Olney -- Jane C Asterbrook   158

Apr   28. 1864   Sylvanus Olney -- Mary Brown   158

May   15, 1864   Newton Robbs -- Nancy Wiett   150

Iron County Marriages
Book " A " 1857-1873

Mav 25, 1864	Alexander N Sloan -- Mrs Margaret H Sloan	88
Jan 14, 1864	Lovel Bryan -- Elvira George	56
Feb 28, 1864	John W Ragen --Deploma Mehala Davidson	140
June 3, 1864	M. S. Wimon -- Almira H Hughs	85
June 12, 1864	William Morgan -- Elizabeth Joiner	45
June 12, 1864	Frederick C Pullam -- Tholida Lagraint	45
June 29, 1864	Jacob Schmith -- Maria Schmith	45
June 28, 1864	William L. Arnold -- Elizabeth Linch	45
June 29, 1864	August Heuring -- Josepha Sturm	45
June 29, 1864	Christian David Kims -- Katherine Weber	45
July 10, 1864	Louis Daire -- Mrs Eliza Parmer	32
May 22, 1864	Edward Holiman -- Matilda Boliner	75
July 6, 1864	William H Chapman-Mrs. Sarah H. Bollock	88
July 5, 1864	Washington Fowler -- Mary Richardson	47
July 7, 1864	Robert F Wood -- Emily N Lukes	4
July 31, 1864	Samuel Rodes -- Susan Jane Arnold	45
May 4, 1864	James Radford -- Elizabeth Howell	149
May 22, 1864	John Ausdon -- Cyntha Parker	149
Aug 3, 1864	James Evans -- Lucy Turner	46
Aug 4, 1864	Frederick Young -- Mary S Quinton	46
July 8 1864	Leonard Turner -- Mrs Lovelia King	163
Aug 4, 1864	William Kruppel -- Caroline Maria Magdalena Engel	57
Aug 18 1864	Benjamin Hendrick--Mrs Parmetia Sanders	46
Aug 21 1864	Quingsoling Collins -- Louisa Quinton	45
Aug 9, 1864	Edward Toohe -- Vinette Aley	45
June 19, 1864	William Henry Vest --Scytha Jane Latham	110

June 9 1864	Samuel P Hampton ---- Virginey Vallie	7
Aug 18, 1864	William Miller --- Frances Brewington	24
Aug 2 1864	James H Waddell -- Mary E Reyburn	161
Mar 30, 1864	George B Jones -- Mary E Taylor	161
Aug 30 1864	Issac N Fake -- Susan Elizabeth Ross	125
July 14, 1864	William M Roberts -- Martha Clementine Flowers	110
July 14, 1864	Mosby West -- Mrs Emily Smith	110
Jan 8. 1864	Eli Horton -- Eaudeely Green	36
Apr 4 1864	Jacob A Goodman -- Polly M Wallace	36
June 27, 1864	John Shaver -- Lucinda Stevenson	36
Dec 15, 1864	James S Hasty --- Catherine Strickland	17
Dec 7, 1864	Joseph Wilson West -- Martha Ann Mayo	24
Dec 19, 1864	Squier C Silvey -- Elizabeth Caroline Quinton	24
Dec 15, 1864	William H Bonney -- Eliza Rauft	57
Dec 18, 1864	Wilhelm Mouser -- Mariette Marks	57
Jan 11, 1865	A D Williams -- Emma M Bailey	163
Jan 14, 1865	Frederick Raths --Doretta Caroline Romer	57
Mar 5, 1865	William Copeland -- Margaret Elizabeth Tubbs	46
Jan. 26, 1865	Carl Boos -- Anne Caroline Mond	57
Mar 9 1865	Lysander Joiner -- Mrs Melissea Gentry	46
Jan 14, 1864?	Charles Edmond -- Martha G Wilson	161
Feb 26 1865	Bird S Smith -- Ann Eliza Taylor	161
Mar 19, 1865	Lot Jointer -- Mrs Amanda Bornes	46
Mar 17 1865	William H Munz --Elizabeth Ann Mitchel	124
Jan 14, 1864?	John David Webb -- Louisa Josephine Fitzpatrick	140
Mar 16, 1865	Robert Alcorn -- Mary Emaline Smith	140

Iron County Marriages
Book " A " 1857-1873

Mar 28, 1865   Philo Fairbrother -- Ann Thompson   46

Mar 29, 1865   Thomas McCabe -- Mrs Ellen Hall   46

Mar. 16, 1865   Thomas Guinin -- Rachel A Daugherty   57

Mar 20, 1865   James Potter -- Sarah Mackland   57

Mar 25, 1865   Frederick Mond -- Marie Kohlhoge   57

Feb 17, 1865   James J Chambers -- Rebecka Freeman   24

Mar 28, 1865   William Crawford -- Mary Caroline C
                                              Redding   24

Mar 20, 1865   Barney Brewington -- Rutha Kenney   24

Apr 7 1865   George W Dale -- Mrs Mary Ann Morris   24

Aug. 28, 1865   Joshua Morris -- Aarena Parker   7

Mar 16, 1865   Robert Thompson -- Artemissa Collins   7

Apr 3, 1865   John Thompson -- Narcissa Collins   7

Jan 1, 1865   William E Jones -- Sarah Poston   125

Mar 26, 1865   Thomas Jones -- Mrs Elizabeth Croley   ?

Mar 20. 1865   Williams Grimes -- Catherine Vickory   75

May 11, 1865   William Folabinbe -- Nancy Howel   88

May 4 1865   S L Hutchens -- Susan Horn   88

Apr 27, 1865   Joseph T Wallace -- Eliza Jane Dale   24

May 4 1865   Jeremiah Vaughn -- Delfa Kelison   24

May 11, 1865   John D Ratliff -- Elizabeth Mayberry   45

July 18. 1864?   Philip Lucus -- Mary M Neely   81

May 13, 1865   John Schwab -- Louisa Rauft   163

Apr 15. 1865   Lewis Daroney -- Sarah E Brock   24

June 13. 1865   Dr Franklin Osburn -- Emiline Priest   163

June 11, 1865   Benjamine F Filley -- Mrs Mahaly
                                              Sutherland   24
Aug 12. 1865   Anthony Kelley -- Harriet Sidge   46

Aug 23. 1865   Henry Valle --Willis Ann [Both Colored] 45

June 4. 1865   I G Clark -- Louisa Strickland   75

June 15, 1865   James Parmer -- Evaline Doshea   75

Aug 17, 1865   Robert Ferguson -- Elizabeth J Raines   75

July 16, 1865   Jefferson G Belmar--Sarah Jane Lashley 103

Aug 6. 1865   Henry Allcock -- Lucinda Elliot   45

Aug 9, 1865   Gottlieb Funk -- Mrs Wilhelmina Jones   45

June 1, 1865   Daniel Dennison -- Elizabeth Grimes   110

June 3. 1865   Henry Sweny -- Sarah Tompson   110

June 3, 1865   Shadwick Flowers -- Susan Sweny   110

Aug. 30, 1865   Thomas Obanon -- Margaret Sloss   103

Jan. 31, 1865   John Willson -- Elizabeth Smith   83
                  [Groom of 7th Kans Cav]
Jan 24, 1865   John W Leonard -- Virginia C Mires   83
                  [Groom of 7th Kans Cav]
Feb 16, 1865   James Mahan -- Mary E Bradshaw   83
                  [Groom of 7th Kans Cav]
Feb 19 1865   John W Ferrier -- Matilda I Skiner   83

July 30, 1865   George W Berner -- Eliza Green   83

Aug 5. 1865   Franklin Bricky -- Susan Bryant
                                     [both colored] 83

Aug 10, 1865   William H. Shanon --Elizabeth Holly   83

Mar 16 1865   Thomas Guinin --Rachel A. Daugherty   57
                  [Groom of London, Eng - Bride of Marshall Co Tn]
Aug 17 1865   Constintine O'Donnel--Emily Jane Bunnyar 24

July 28, 1865   William Burt -- Harriet Bunnyard   24

Aug 14 1865   Qualiv Sights-Mrs Hester Ann Berrington 83
                  [Children Amanda , Mahala and Willis Sights]
Aug 24 1865   David Armes -- Morning Howington   83
                       [Son Westly Armes]
Aug 27, 1865   Lewis Robitt -- Harriet Choice   83
                  [Children Mariah Ann. Cooley and Martha Robitt]
Aug 27, 1865   Mark Cooley -- Harriet Walden   83
                  [Children Samuel Andy and Quence Cooley]
Aug 29 1865   Artimus Green -- Caroline Fax   83
                  [Children Ann. Elizabeth. Amanda & Washington Green]
Aug 30. 1865   Jesse Warren -- Dilly Smith   83

18

[Children   Jane and Green Warren]

Aug 30, 1865   James Hunt -- Frances Berriman   83
     [Children. Issac, George and Francis Norton]
Aug 30, 1865   Henry Banks -- Siller Cauldwell   83
     [Children. George, Sarah, Sinta and Susan Cauldwell]
Aug 30, 1865   Robert Wilson -- Jemima Cuning   83
     [Children. Hannah and Mary K Wilson]
Sept 6, 1865   William White -- Mary Ruebottom   83

Sept 6, 1865   Jeremiah Spencer -- Sabina Ingram   83
[Children Susan, Andrew, John H , Fisbey E , Martha H.
                          and George R]
Aug 7, 1865   John W Palmer -- Mrs Elizabeth Wimpy   7

Sept. 8, 1865   Issac Moore--Rosanna Smith [both colored]46

Sept. 14, 1865   Joseph Ellis -- Nancy Clapper   46

Sept 10, 1865   Thomas J Davidson -- Jane Davis   24

Sept 27, 1865   Steve Creth -- Lucy Creth   119

Sept 29 1865   Miles Stevens -- Jane Stevens   119

July 27, 1865   Warren E Peck -- Elizabeth C. Berryman 17

July 27, 1865   William V Sitton -- Nancy Rea   17
     [Groom of Lincoln Co   bride of wayne Co]
Aug 2, 1865   Charles Thompson -- Elizabeth Miller   24
     [Bride the widow of Daniel S Miller desc]
Sept 28, 1865   James Groves -- Mary Elizabeth Burnyard 24

Sept 28, 1865   Michael Spitsmiller -- Louisa Turnbough 24

Oct 5. 1865   William W Waters -- Mrs Forby Williams 24

Sept. 14, 1865   F Napier -- Mrs Nelly Healy   45

Oct 1 1865   Joseph Seitz -- Lilly Ann McFadden   45

Oct. 21, 1865   John Burch -- Martha K Jones   45

July 7, 1865   William J Donally -- Sophia Jane Day   155

Oct 20, 1865   Edward Fogs -- Tena Harris   119
     [One child Alexd Harris]
Oct 24, 1865   John Groves -- American Ethington   46

Oct 22 1865   D F Martin -- Emma Franks   17

May 7, 1865   Thomas E Crocker -- Marinda Crocker   85

Oct 22 1865   Joseph Dixon Lloyd -- Elmira Sorpherra

O"Neil   48

Sept   14, 1865   John Washington Counts -- Fannie
                                    Josephine Young 48

Apr   27, 1865   Jessee Brown -- Emaline Martin   140

June   4 1865   Madison Allcorn -- Nerussa Hunt   140

Nov   8. 1865   John Kitchell -- Martha L Duty   85

Nov   26. 1865   David Kaffer -- Cinty Ellen Douglass   45

Sept   14, 1865   Daniel P Anderson -- Martha Ann Davis   163

Oct   21, 1865   Charles L. Thompson -- Melinda R A
                                             Compton 163

Oct   26, 1865   James A Keltner -- Mary L Gibson   163

Nov   6 1865   Josiah Henson -- Mrs Nancy Buford   163

Nov   20. 1865   Amos H Hunt -- Elizabeth A Allison   17
Nov   28 1865   John Armstrong -- Charity Dickens   76

Oct   31, 1865   Henry Thomas -- Ann Edison   76
Nov   14 1864?   John Scritchfield -- Elizabeth Dyer   11

Jan   6, 1866   Ephraim Hasty -- Martha Merricks   40

Jan   14 1866   William F Lee -- Lucy Steel   46

Jan   18, 1866   George Barbut -- Martha Edington   45

Jan   7 1866   Elias T Reed -- Ann Lee   45

Nov   29, 1865   Joseph John Moyer -- Adaline Chilton   88
                   [groom of Iron Co., bride of Shannon Co]
Nov   16, 1865   Thomas Emboden -- Sinthy Nealy   88

Jan   28 1866   Newton J Arnold -- Ellen Thorp   66

Feb   12. 1866   John McFadden -- Martha Head   66

Dec   10 1865   William Johnson -- Nancy Thompson   110

Dec   21, 1865   Urbin Sample -- Mrs Martha Asher   110

Feb   13 1866   George Woods -- Melinda Sweeny   47

Feb   26, 1866   William Williams -- Sarah E Murray   46

Feb   27 1866   William B Messer -- Narcissa Read   121
                   [groom of Iron Co , bride of Madison Co

Iron County Marriages
Book " A " 1857-1873

Mar 12, 1866   Henry Vasterling -- Johana Ahrens   57

Mar 26, 1866   Peter Evans -- Martha Fass   47

Jan 1, 1866   John R. Adams -- Delacy A Mason   87

Apr 11, 1866   John R Higdon -- Rachel Lashley   17

Feb 1, 1866   David F. Edwards -- Mary L. Thompson   163
                [Groom of Butler Co. , bride of Iron Co]
Mar. 21, 1866   Samuel R Kelley -- Mary J Philips   163
                [Groom of Ste Genevieve Co , bride of Iron Co.]
Apr. 11, 1866   Marion Kelly [freedman]-- Willis Ann
                        [both colored]   Guyto 163
Apr. 5, 1866   Abraham W. Knees -- Mary C Cox   88

May 1, 1866   Jacob Elliott -- Mary Walker   45

Apr 15, 1866   G W. Lashley -- Nancy J. Mires   75

Apr 29, 1866   Eli Detherew -- Nancy Forster   45

Apr. 26, 1866   Thomas Elliott -- Mary Louise Moore   45

Nov 1, 1865?   Andrew Mathews -- Eggy Carter   47

Nov 11, 1866?   James Ellis -- Adaline Carter   47

Mar 4, 1866   Robert Dunn -- Matilda Seal   75

May 6, 1866   Jefferson Thomas -- Jane Donohue   142
                [both colored]
Jan 28, 1866   James Monroe Fitzpatrick -- Margaret
                             [Gollerhugh [Gallaher] 88
                [Groom of Iron Co , bride of Reynolds Co]
Feb 22, 1866   William Newberry --Frances Johns   88

Dec. 7, 1865   Isham Andrew -- Melinda Whitner   163
                [Late Slaves Ch John Henry and William Calvin]
Jan 28, 1866   James A Chapman -- Mary Ann Wood   85

June 24 1865   Mathew Hurt --Mrs Catherine Hasty   110

Jan 11, 1866   Albert Braeur--Wilhelmine Zute   163

April 17, 1865 Anthony Alexander Farrar-Catherine Buckner
                                                         163
[Late slaves Children,Ellen Emiline & Lewis Alfred Farrar]
Sept 17, 1865 Sydney Bollinger--Phebe Smith [late slaves]
                                                         163
Sept. 19, 1865 Reubin Wyatt-Amanda Bugg [late slaves]163
                [children Mary Alice and Amanda Elizabeth]

Sept 23, 1865 Green Blanks--Amy Caldwell [late slaves

Iron County Marriages
Book " A " 1857-1873

children Lucy, Alvin, Tinah, Harriet-taken by rebels] 163

Oct 1, 1865   Edmond Collier--Charlotte Friar [late slaves
Children Hannah, Henry, Lewis Jane, Mason and Daniel]163

Nov 30, 1865   George Carter-Nancy Whitener [late slaves]
                                                              163

Mar 18, 1866   William Riley Skiles--Mrs Sarah Thomison110

April 8, 1866   James Flowers-- Mary Lane   110

July 4, 1866   Elijah Kelly-- Martha Waldon [colored] 46

April 26, 1866   Jerome C Nall--Mrs Mary E Imboden   17

May 13, 1866   James M Ashlock--Mirantha A Lashley   17

May 21, 1866   Thomas N Berryman--Mrs Coreya D Wyatt 17

April 6, 1866   John Burden--Viny Stephens   5

June 23, 1866   William Robbs--Mrs Nancy Guffey   45

July 24, 1866   -----Longgreat--Harriet Burch   66
[g age 24 bride 21 years Wit James Groves & Lambert Webster
May 20, 1866   William Sizemore-- Olive Cowan   61

Aug 6 1866   Eli D Ake--Jane S Bradbury   61

May 15, 1866   Alexander Robs--Elizabeth Williams   75

June 14, 1866   J S Vicory--M S Elders   75

June 17, 1866   William Bone--Aney Albridge   75

June 24, 1866   Jefferson Millener--Rachael J Prough   88

Aug 7 1866   George Brock--Malinda Grigsby [both colored]
[g age 24 bride 30 yrs Wit Henry Merrill & M stevens]66

July 9, 1866   Columbus J Beckett--Mary T Dougan   56

July 15 1866   John H kenner--Martha Blankenship   17

Aug 26, 1866   Ludwig Schmidt--Mrs ' Magdalena Pfeil   57
[Wit william C Rauft & Andrew Woerner]
June 26, 1866   John Allridge--Louisa Goodwin   75

Aug 27, 1866   William J Crosslan--Susan Swaringamed   75
            [g of " Ran " Co B of Iron Co]
June 3 1866   John McFagen--Elisa Craven   112

Aug 2, 1866   John Wallis--Charita Ann Loid   112

22

Aug 26, 1866   Dale Piles--Commensa Loid   112

June 21, 1866   Alexander S Moore--Elizabeth Jane Cain 163

July 12, 1866   J L Banes--M Malinda Furgason   75

Sept. 30, 1866   John H Harris--Mary J Haywood   112

Oct. 11, 1866   Thomas H Snyder--Mary Adaline Tullock   45

Sept 23, 1866   George Thomas-- Judy Dickens [colored]142

Oct. 11, 1866   Jacob Harris--Mary McFarland [colored]142

Aug 5, 1866   Geo W Hartgroves--Missouri Jane Vest   85

Nov 1, 1866   Abraham Zimmerman--Elizabeth E Reek   46

Oct. 4, 1866   Joseph Thompson--Jane A Hale   88

Aug. 20, 1866   George W Cox--Mary A Richmand   88

Sept 18, 1866   Andrew J Reyburn--Frances H Bruce [unsigned]

Nov 8, 1866   George W Wallace--Lucinda Wilson   66
[g age 41, bride 25 Wit, M.L. Claybaugh & J.M Reed]

Aug 18, 1866   Aaron Conley--Elizabeth Turner   73

Sept 8 1866   Benjamine Warsing-Mrs Elizabeth Scotchfield
                                                           45
Nov 8, 1866   Dunkin Arnett--Lois Jane Smith   17

Oct 23, 1866   William G.R Shultz--Myra Hunt   17
                 [both of Wash. Co]
Sept 5, 1866   Andrew White--Mary Shaeffer   163

Sept. 11, 1866 Archibald G McMurty-Missouri Ann Wyatt 163
      [groom of Wayne Co Bride Of Iron Co]
Oct 16, 1866   Lafayette Praul-- Eliza Warner   163
      [groom of Wash. Co - bride of Iron Co]
Aug 30, 1866   John Mairten--Mary Oen   74

Dec 3 1866   Caire Smith--Adeline Dunn   75

Oct 25, 1866   Huston Seal--Mary Dunn   75

Nov 23, 1866   Henry Richhter--Mrs Johanna Marie   45
                                 Fredericka Martin
Nov 11, 1866   Cyrus A Raney--Harriet McColough   112

Oct 4, 1866   Joe Madkins-- Angeroney Gideon   121

Nov 17, 1866   Fredreick W Kohlhage--Mary A Elser   45

Nov 15, 1866   Joseph Huff --Martha J Mayfield   45
    [groom of Ironton -bride Golcoda Il]
Sept 6, 1866   David Prough--Sarah Hawkins   73

Nov 11 1866   Harice k Taylor--Mary t Neighbors   73

Nov 1, 1866   Samuel S Fergusson--Margaret Bates   45

Aug 23 1866   Charles M. Peel--Martha Gibson   61

Nov 21, 1866   Harvey Turnbow--Cynthia A Satterfield   143

Dec 10 1866   Levy Cline --Amanda Jane Walden   113
    [g age 22, b age 20 both of Clark Co Wit Levy Cline Sr
            and Lorence Whener]
Dec 25, 1866   Jos Reubottom--Jane Kinkade   142

Jan 2, 1867   Henry Merrill--Matilda Stevens   142

Jan 4, 1867   Samuel Perry --Rebecca Chandler   45

Jan 24. 1867   John Caseboult--Susana Holt   6

Dec 6, 1866   John Croy --Eliza Nalle   17
    [groom of Wayne Co , bride of Iron Co
Feb 13, 1867   Elam Adcison Slone-Rebecca Jane Stevenson13
    [groom of Wash Co , bride of Iron Co]
Feb 13 1867   Nelson Creath--Laura Creath   119
    [one son 5 yrs old named Charley]

Dec 3, 1866   Thomas Howard--Elizabeth Rubel   121

Dec 23 1866   Thomas Bates --Mary Seile   121

Jan 6, 1867   William H Danels---- Harriet J Hues   121

Feb 6 1867   William M Evans--Sarah Ann Stephens   143

Mar 3 1867   James Beckett--Amarilla Berryman   45

Mar 28 1867   Reuben Sumpter--Caroline Hawk   10

Dec 28. 1866   Samuel Kelly--Amanda ,Thomasson   163

Jan 20, 1867   Edward Harrison --Caroline Sides   163

Jan 2, 1867   Noah Blankenship--Mary Barton   163

Feb 21 1867   Gustavus Rahm--Caroline Dettmar   113
    [Wit Adolph Dettmer & Phillip Kolb]
Feb 20 1867   James L Cline--Mary M Montgomery   113
    [Wit Samuel E Carlton & John W Handcock

Iron County Marriages
Book " A " 1857-1873

Mar 6, 1867   Reason M Neill--Hannah Childers   113
     [Wit Reason M Gunnett & Susan Ketcherside]
Mar 7, 1867   Benard Rutschman-- Maria Breitenatein   113
     [Wit James Anthony & Charles Morgan]
Feb 25, 1867   Gideon Baughman--Mrs narissa hudleston 128

Feb 17, 1867   Andrew Lewis--Angaline Rose   112

Jan 16, 1867   Jasper Shrum--Elizabeth McNail   88

Mar 24, 1867   James P Keath-- Marie Kemble   93

Mar 30, 1867   William B Palmer--Sarah Dickson   112

Mar 21 1867   William E Chilton--Mary Williams   112

Mar 27, 1867   James R Rucker--Eveline C Barger   160

Mar 25, 1867   James Denny-- Frances Rivers   113
     [Wit. Nancy Cline & Washington Cline]
April 4, 1867   Allen Nicholas--Jemima E. Thompson   113
     [Wit. James Groves & Mary E Groves]
April 27 1867   Joseph M. Reeves--Elizabeth Litrell   113
     [Wit. Charles W. Norris & Joseph Litrell]
May 12, 1867   Alfred Brimingham-Mrs Sarah Jane Phillips45

April 4, 1867   Valentine Robison--Mary Salina Brewer   46

Mar 11, 1867   Robert Muse--Nancy Norris   88

Mar 31, 1867   James Faulkingberry--Ellen Copeland   88
     [Both of Reynolds County]
April 4, 1867   George Orie--Eliza A Rice   88

May 5, 1867   George H. W Miller--Mrs Mary Crownover 128

Feb 23, 1867   Thomas Joiner--Jemima Mead   67

July 23, 1867   William Death--Amorett O. Mead   90

May 3, 1867   James Dudley--Sarah Timmons   61

May 11 1867   August Appel--Dorothea Dettman   113
     [Wit August Heinrichs & Charles Martin]
June 24 1867   Williams Reeves -- Martha Barbett   ,   113
     [Wit Alfred Proffit & John Groves]
June 23, 1867   Martin Breaton--Ellen O'Donnell   145
June 23, 1867   Michael Tierney--Catherine Whaler   145

June 23, 1867   John Webb --Nancy E Moore   110

June 23, 1867   Albert D Williamson--Louisa Hartzell   110
     [groom of Miami Co. Ohio bride of Iron Co]
April 4, 1867   William Reel-- Ann Proffit   61

Iron County Marriages
Book " A " 1857-1873

[Wit. William Williams & James Dudley
June 30, 1867   A K Burnett--Miss Lindsay   61

July 4, 1867   Thomas Johnson--Lizzie Cooper   61

Jan 8. 1867   Phillip Kolb--Emilie Hickeritz   72

April 4, 1867   Philip Hofmeister--Julia Engel   72
      [Wit Frederick Will 7 John Engel]
Aug 3, 1867   Henry Barsche--Emeline Schoen   45

June 9, 1867   Jesse Campbell--Mary Ann Kearns   45

May 2, 1867   D D Emmons --Mrs Josie H Hall   163
      [groom of Wayne Co ,bride of Iron Co.]
May 28, 1867   Azariah Martin --Mattie M Hill   163

May 17, 1867   Henry Walden--Matilda Mary Whitener 163
      [groom of Wash Co , bride of Iron Co.]
July 7, 1867   Samuel Boyd--Angeline Kelly   163

Aug 16, 1867   George Taylor-- Elizabeth Turner   67

June 20 1866?   John P Huff--Emeline Seal   75

Aug 11, 1867   Thomas Gibson--Caroline Helm   164

Mar 10 1867   James Meders--Elizabeth Gemerson   120
      [One of Wash Co , other of Iron Co]
Sept. 1, 1867   William Bogus--Adolin Anderson   67

Sept 1, 1867   Henry Wood--Sarah Ann McGarnigan   45

July 30, 1867   Evans Crico--Molisy Hurt?   88
      [groom of Dent Co , bride of Iron Co]
July 11, 1867   John Newton--Margaret Melvina O'Bannon 77

Oct 17, 1867   John Dean--Sarah L Godard   67

April 3 1867   James Therman--Margaret Miller   56

Oct 14, 1867   Isaac Foister--Adeline 1 Gibson   56

Sept 8 1867   Levi H Webb--Melissa Wood   56

Oct 29, 1867   Jonathan Justice--Mrs Cassinda Doyle 46

Oct 30 1867   John Evans--Jemima Nichols   142

Oct 31, 1867   Adam Ward--Julia Thompson   142

Nov 11 1867   Daniel Sutton--Sarah A Young   128

Oct 31, 1867   Henry Lashley--Elizabeth Tullock   45

26

Nov 1, 1867   Hezakiah Ragsdale--Sally Revis   112

Nov 17, 1867   Peter B Kinckel--Nancy S. Hickman   112

Dec 8, 1866?   Elias Horton-- Eliza Ann Latham   45

Dec 12 1866?   Chistopher Colubus St John--
                                   Subrina H Kelly   45
Sept 12 1866? Thomas J Lee--Mariah E Morgan   166
         [married in Stoddard Co   recorded in Iron Co   ]

May 13 1866?   David Marler --Cassey Elliott   45

May 21, 1866?   John C Burk--Frances McCallum   45

Nov 3, 1867   Henry Bock-- Wilhelmina Jorris   72
         [wit Henry Temme & Johanne Jorris]

July 13, 1867   Henry Bartlebaugh--Polly Ann Jones   113
         [wit Mary Ann Jones & A. M M Louisa Rauft]

Sept 4, 1867   William W Ferguson--Mary H Miller   88

Nov 17, 1867   C H William -- Mahala A Sutterfield   143

Nov 17, 1867   Andrew Sullivan-- Mary Eunice Gaston   110

Sept 8 1867   Thomas Richarson--Nancy Flowers   110

Dec 5, 1867   Henry Johnson -- Angeline Snyder   45

Sept 17 1867 W R McFadden-- Mary E Miller   163
         [groom of Wayne Co , bride of Iron Co   ]
Oct   14, 1867   Edgar W. Pease--Harriett H Burch   113
         [Wit Harriet Burch & Mary A Burch]
Dec 23, 1867   James Pitman --Betty Jackson   113
         [Wit Mona Ormes & Jemima Bollinger]
Jan 1. 1868   Frederick Amoldy?--Mary A Russell   113
         [Wit A Dettman & Philip Kolb]
Dec 31, 1867   Ortery Flowers--Sarah Jane Scarbrough   60

Jan 5 1868   Madison C Farr--Malissa B Hughes   11

Dec 24 1867   William P. Herald --Adia Guliver   88
         [groom of Reynolds Co , bride of Iron Co   ]
Dec 10 1867   John Goggin--Louiza Sloan   88
         [groom of Reynolds Co , bride of Iron Co   ]

Dec 3, 1867   George D Slone--Elizabeth Roop   88

Mar 10, 1868   William Hancock--Mrs Mary A Fooks   103

Nov 15 1867   William Robbs--Nancy Huff   75

Dec 8, 1867   Caven L Hartman--Miss L R   Edmmunds   67

Jan 4, 1867   Herman Arnold --Eva Rahm   72
          [Wit Joseph Rauft & Fritz Peetz
Feb 2, 1868   John Davidson--Nancy Sutton   128

Feb 18 1868   William Ake--Mrs Anna E Walker   45

Feb 7, 1868   W B Brille--Mary T Austin   84
          [groom of Fredericktown. bride of Arcadia]
Feb 24, 1868   Marida M. Riddle--Sarah J Snow   112

Jan 28 1868   Harrison Sweeny--Mrs Angeline Rawlings   110

Feb 20, 1868   Peter Cox--Ann Carter   88

Mar 8, 1869   Lewis L Burch--Hannah C Bartley   113

Mar 17, 1868   Squire Alexander Pooley--Sarah Chappel   45

Mar 5, 1868   Joseph Hasty--Catherine Shrum   84

Mar 5, 1868   Benjamine C Walker--Nancy Conway   144

Mar 23 1868   John Buckner--Caroline Brown   113
          [Wit Ferdinand Schmitz & Louise Rauft]
Feb 23, 1868   Richard Roeslein-- Martha E Sinclair   128

Mar 6, 1868   D B Lee-- Mary A Shrum   88

Mar 5, 1869?   John Q Tyrrel--Margaret J Casey   67
          [filed Jan 26, 1870]
Oct 27 1865? Eli Detheron--Nancy Foster   45
          [Filed Oct 29, 1865]
Oct 29 1868   John S Luthy--Sarah E. Gravum   163
          [Filed Jan 8, 1869]
Oct 29 1868   James W Moser--Visa A Gravum   163
          [Filed Jan 8, 1869]
Nov 12. 1868   Alexander Sherrill--Lydia L C. Jackson   163
          [Filed Jan 8 1869]
Nov 19, 1868   George W Cole --Mrs Sarah J Henson   163
          [Filed Jan 8, 1869]
Jan 1, 1869?   Henry Coldwell--Ellen Russell   163
          [Filed April 14, 1868?]
Mar 26, 1868   William P Clayton--Polly Ann Kirkland   88
          [Filed April 2, 1868]
Mar 15, 1868   James P Adams-- Mary P Campbell   88
          [Filed April 2, 1868]
Mar 26, 1868   James Morgan--Elizabeth Warsham   88
          [filed April 9, 1868]
April 13 1868 Jacob W Funk--Martha Pease   163

Feb 16, 1868   John King--Mrs Caroline Grass   72

Iron County Marriages
Book " A " 1857-1873

April 8, 1868   John H. Delano--Mattie Harvey   15

April 27, 1868   Joseph H Thompson--Keziay Legrand   113

April 2, 1868   Christopher C Russell--
                            Artimeisa M Collins   112
May 3, 1868   John Beckman--Isabella Gilliam   45

May 5 1868   Charles F Morgan--Emily F Will   72

May 28, 1868   August Reckert--Doretha Peetz   72

June 5, 1868   Wilson Farmer --Melvina Horton   113
        [Wit. E Horton & Samuel Warsing]
Dec 25, 1867   Samuel T Gay --Mary Ann Newman   163

April 19, 1867   John S Scagg--Sarah Rebecca Moser   163

May 24, 1868   L F Dill--Drisciler Moore   67

July 9, 1868   Daniel Paulas--Marcha Campbell   45

July 25, 1868   William Moore--Pauline Colston   45

April 26, 1868   Andrew Cooley-- Frances Reves   75

Aug 9 1866?   Mike Kauffman-- Margaret Mangel   46

Oct 21, 1867?   Jacob A Roop -- Mary J Valley   88

Oct 22, 1867?   William S. George-- Sarah J Roop   88

Oct 8, 1868   Issac Sutton --Mary Rohdes   95

Aug 20, 1868   William Jackson -- Susan Marlow   112

Aug 6, 1868   William G Fairchild--Mattie J Grigsby   17

Mar 11. 1868   George S Kinkead--Fannie Blanton   17
        [groom of St Francois Co , bride of Iron Co]
July 2 1868   William H H Thomas--Rebecca A Brill   163
        [groom of Jefferson Co , bride of Iron Co
July 9. 1868   Reuben Wyatte--Lucy Jane Martin   163

Nov 20, 1868   Alexander White--Margaret Russell   141

------------   William G Delts--Miss C M Donaldson   46
        [filed Oct 20, 1868]
Aug 2, 1868   George Hampton--Jane Johnson   121

Nov 26, 1868   F T Peck--Mary Andress   46

Aug 15, 1868   J. A W. Russell--Catherine Bell   110

Nov 21 1868   Thomas Sparge --Rachel A M Johnson   110

Nov 1, 1868   James B Shelton--Mary P Sanders   88

Dec 23 1868   W A Palmer--Phebe A Newman   46

Jan 14, 1869   Martin Dienst--J Bourgin   67
       [groom of Iron Co , bride of Ste Genevieve Co]
Dec 26, 1869   N H Haller --Sophia Essenwien   45
       [Recorded Jan 12 1868 One of these two dates must be
         wrong, most likely the marriage date [1869 should
      read 1868]
Dec 18, 1868   George J Moerkel--Mary C Kleinigus   72

Jan 26, 1869   Lambert Webster--Hannah Hall   45

Jan 1 1869   John Roth--Mary Catherina Hall   45

Feb 10, 1869   A W Coleman --Julia Peck   163

Sept 27, 1868 Lewis Shelton --Mrs Jemima Bollinger   163
     [groom of Jefferson Co , bride of Iron Co--both Colored]
Jan 17 1869   John Clemmons-- Mary Smith   60

Sept 10, 1868   George Camel-- Mary Seal   75

Sept 10 1868   W M Scrogins--Carlin Huff   75

Oct 25, 1868   W M Scrogins Mary J Pinkly   75

Mar 5, 1869   William Ruble--Hepsiba Lewis   121

Dec 20, 1868   William F McColley--Florence Taylor   139

Dec 25 1868   Robert Tilley--Ann Heckleman   139

Dec 24 1868   William Johnson-- Rebeca Loyd   112

Jan 10 , 1869   George Blank-- Matilda Beard   142

Jan 12 1869   James Barger-- Mary Sloan   13

Feb 21 1869   Silas Caldwell-Mrs Jane Merrill [colored]142

Jan' 31, 1869   Michail Clary--Margarett Ryan   96

April 8 1869   John Hovy--Catherine Othman   96

Feb 16, 1869   H B Henderson--Sarah T Adams   2

Feb 28 1869   Edward Newberry--Sophia Edmons   88

April 6, 1869   Arnold Ridanny?--Mary A Schreckenbert   96

Mar 17, 1869   Jesse F Derrick--Elizabeth Jane Inman   45

Feb 9 1869   James George --Hellen Miller   77

April 25, 1869   James Mabery--Betty Jane Phillips   77

April 29, 1869   Samuel Andrews Jr --Sophia Wert Miller   118
[groom of Wayne Co , md. at residence of father of bride]
May 6, 1869   Timothy O'Neil--Mrs Mary Jones   46

April 25, 1869   Billings Harris--Eastatia Deguire   92

Mar 28, 1869   Stephen Bourgouis-Mary Axelandrie Legrand 92

June 5, 1869   Thomas H B Polk--Mrs Sarah Jane Irvan 92

July 25, 1869   Austin A Deguire--Eliza Spangler   92

Aug 1, 1869   L O O'Neader--Mary Russell   121

Aug 16, 1869   Thomas Diggs--July Garrett   141

Aug 19, 1869   Samuel A. Stevenson--Artelis Hubble   128

April 8, 1869   John W Whitworth--Drucilla E Tong   17

Aug 21, 1869   Charles O Fairchild--Sallie A Grigsby   17

July 4, 1869   Andrew Winn--Juley Sinclar   121

Sept 2, 1869   Thomas Bergman--Mary Spragly   112

Sept 5, 1869   William Adams--Ann McNail   88
[both of Reynolds County]
June 10, 1869   Joseph B Wallis --Sarah Corder   19

Sept 5, 1869   A Keathly--Nancy Jane Asbury   77

Aug 28, 1869   Jacob Groves--Mrs Harriet Berch   45

Sept 15, 1869   Theodore McKenney--Isabella Reyburn   13

Oct 17 1869   Robert Creath--Sarah Creath   141

July 4, 1869   William Cassaday--Kath Dearmint   139

Sept 16 1869   James K P Dilts--Josey R Ringer   17

Nov 24, 1869   L T Hine--Fida A Terrill   46

Oct 29, 1869   Josiah Campbell--Mary Woodroe   45

Oct 30, 1869   Albert L Lakey--Kate House   134

Iron County Marriages
Book " A " 1857-1873

Sept 23, 1869   Esau Stephens--Mary Nix   88

Oct   3 1869   Andrew J Randels--C E   Marten   112

Nov   14, 1869   Joseph Rauft--Magdalene Schneider   53

Dec   29, 1869   Nelson Evans --Nancy Harris   141

Dec   29, 1869   Frank Smith --Sarah Blanks   141

Sept 5, 1869   E Clark -- Nancy J Smith   128

Dec   16, 1869   William P Kirkland --Fannie Smith   4

Dec   26, 1869   William P Helton --Eliza Ann O'Bannon   8
      [groom of Wash Co ; bride of Iron Co]
Dec   10, 1869   Jakile Hampton Forehand--Cansady Mabery   77

July 15, 1869   Dillard Terly--Narcessus Huff   116

Dec   10, 1869   Moses McNail- Sarah R Mills   88

Dec   2 1869   Peter Ake--Mollie Boswell   162

Oct   20, 1869   John C McDaniel--Margaret A Messer   115

Jan   22, 1870   Daniel Jordon--Amy Ludy   141

Jan   20, 1870   William M Woolem--Henrietta Pollard   45

Mar   5, 1870   John Q Tyrrel--Margaret J Cayce   67

Dec   19 1869   Charles Holloman--Margaret Tullock   142

Feb   10, 1870   Peter Hartgrove--Mary Miller [not signed]

Feb   28, 1870   John H. Valley--Sarah J Albright   65

Mar   5 1870   Levi Flourz--Santee M Guffey   45

Mar   13 1870   Jefferson Parker--Sarah Frances Miller   70

Mar   10, 1870   Johann Michael Walter --Maria Grandhhomme   45

Feb   27 1870   James Highly--Sarah E Rice   88

Jan   25, 1870   Stephen Anderson--Martha Knit   22

Feb   6, 1870   John Phillip--Missouri E Harrison   77

Mar   13, 1870   Alfred G Pullam--Margaret Statler   93

Mar   17, 1870   Thomas Calahan--Mary Jane Bell   154

Date	Names	Page
Mar 23, 1870	Noah Arisman --Martha M Webb	154
Mar 17, 1870	George Bailey--Eliza Carter	37
April 19, 1870	William E. Bell--Lucy A George	88
Feb 17, 1870	Robert Miller--Zaury Elizabeth Canaday	37
Feb 21, 1870	Henry Miller --Sarah Ann Canaday	37
Feb 28, 1870	Hewitt Dennis--Martha Fleeman	37
May 5, 1870	Charles Arnett--Mrs Caroline Dyer	45
Feb 17, 1870	Emanuel Seltser --Nancy Jane Farris	110
May 2, 1870	James Martin --Mary A Ivia	146
April 24, 1870	Andrew G Palmer --Ann Ketcheson	18
April 14, 1870	Elias Volner--Margaret A Richeson	18
April 3, 1870	Thomas James --Martha Jane Smyth?	18
July 27, 1870	John McLain--Mary Ann Bershur	45
June 26, 1870	Benjamine Davidson--Catherine Farrar	142
April 19, 1870	Benjamine Campbell--Mary C Myres	121
June 6, 1870	Marshall Smith Petty-Margaret Jane Irvin	88
Mar 31, 1870	William M. Madkins--Julcy Ann F Cofman	121
April 14, 1870	Thomas Milard --Mary R. Treace	121
April 21, 1870	Pinkney F Collins--Carolyne Issibell Smith	128
Aug 8, 1870	Frederick Radach--Julia Thiel	45
Sept 27 1870	Lewis Beachman--Maggie Dickard	119
Sept. 11, 1870	Samuel L Beeman--M A Mayfield	25
Sept 4 1870	Edward Wall--Mary Lester	63
Sept 4 1870	Thomas Rategan--Susan Lester	63
July 3 1870	John Harrison --Euritty Usrey	48
Sept 29 1870	Amos P Westfall--Mary Jane Berch	93
Oct 4 1870	Ferges Sloan --Mary Ann Thomas	13

Oct   5   1870   Lorenzo D Carl--Sarah Hood   13

Oct   22, 1870   Edmond Aubuchon --Amanda Cooper   141

Sept 11. 1870   Andrew J Bruer--Mary Johnson   112

Aug   7, 1870   James Stevenson--Artilisey Stephenson   48

Oct   9, 1870   Moses J Hanks--Louisa Taylor   51

Oct   5   1870   William Hanks--Manerva Winn   51

Nov   3, 1870   Thomas Green-- Elizabeth Harberson   154

Aug   28, 1870   J W Hutchins--Sariah C O'Neal   121

Aug   7. 1870   Charles E Smith--Annie Colans   121

Aug   28, 1870   Buril T Hickman--Ashsh? E. Chilton   121

Nov   6. 1870   James Lewis --Lucinda Wallis   112

Oct   11, 1870   Ephraim Vaughn--Catherine Moris   35
      [groom of Butler Co · bride of Iron Co
Oct   25, 1870   Lewis Highly --Ann Baker   110

Nov   9 1870   James Vaughn--Mrs Susan Smith   110

Nov   23, 1870   Peter J Callahan--Mary A Gibson   46

Sept 11, 1870   James Adams--Elizabeth Mason   22

Dec   22, 1870   John Peace--Obediance A Lashley   77

Dec   18, 1870   Rally Chilton--Polly Jane Roberts   112

Oct   30, 1870   John L Long--Celestis Isabell Spangler   128
      [groom of Illinois bride of Iron Co]
July 17, 1870   Alfred Yankey--Barbara A Hildebrand   116

Oct   27 1870   Noah A Seigman--Malinda E Bounce   45

Oct   37 1370   John b Evans--Charity Mountain Creath   45

Oct   28 '1870   John W Fagan--Sarah M Martin   45

Nov   30. 1870   Carl Kassemacher--Sophia Eisenwein   45

Dec   4, 1870   James Carr--Rebecca J Mateney   45

Dec   4   1870   John Cora--Sarah Weble   45

Jan   1   1871   L W Burgan--Mary Jane Huff   45

Jan 4 1871   W A Lyman -- Cornelia l Hyden   41
     [groom of State of Kansas; bride of Iron Co]
Dec 15 1870   John W Pearce--Seany Davis   22

Dec. 25, 1870   Robert Atkins --Sarah J Stanton   22

Jan 1, 1871   John A Harper --Elizabeth m Compton   22

Jan. 29, 1871   James W. Andis --Calvaney Wallis   71

Nov 21, 1870   Francis Beal--Margaret Shoer   27

Dec. 10, 1870   Robert Kirk--Elizabeth E. Love   4

Dec 29, 1870   Jesse D Terley--Demerrius Huff   105

Feb 11, 1871   John C. Horton--Caroline F. Brewer   46

Sept 27, 1870   Edward F Barrow --Elizabeth C Peck   17
     [groom late of Galveston, Texas]
Feb 20. 1871   William W Swadley--Mary E Ryan   63

Feb 21, 1871   William C Thomas--Julia A W Miller   41

Mar 7 1871   John Timlin--Rosa Lucinda Horton   71

Feb 2, 1871   John Sutton--Irenia Highly   54
          [groom of Wash Co   bride of Iron Co]

May 10, 1852?   James P Walker--Mary Cochran   55
     [married at Walnut Post Office Indenpendance Co, Ark]
Mar 26, 1871   Joseph Danley--Ellen Campbell   46

Mar 15, 1871   Charles A Smith--Anna L Bishop   41

April 9, 1871   George W. Lando--Nelly C Green   1

Mar 20, 1871   Cornelius Sutton--Adline Spangler   128

April 15, 1871   William Russell--Martha C Keach   41

April 30, 1871   James Strumbaugh--Mrs Eliza Hughes   45

Feb 16, 1871   Durne L Hilderbrand--Mary E Miller   128

April 15, 1871   Louis Derry--Mary Ann Warren   68

Feb 19, 1871   James J Lankiston--Marenia A Dickson 152

Mar 5, 1871   Charles C Jones--Nancy Ruble   152

Mar --1871   William W Close--Nancy J Wilson   75

May 3, 1871   John F Club --Julia Ann Boatright   71

April 15, 1871   John Perry--Sarah Yater   71

April 4, 1871   James W Cole --Mary J. Bryan   56

Nov 30, 1868?   Christopher C. Taylor --Eliza Brooks   56
      [filed May 18, 1871]
Dec 19, 1871   Henry Wright--Elizabeth Brogean   56

April 13, 1871   W M Cunningham -- Elizabeth R Brown   110

Mar 12 1871   Robert Thompson-- Margaret Akers   110

April 19, 1871   David W Dickson--Artemisa Brady   112

Jan 14, 1869?   H W Janes--Jane Bollinger   75

Mar 3, 1871   John Buckner--Nancy Brown   75

Dec. 25, 1870   William Willett--Susan Bollinger   43

May 18, 1871   Zacrier F Kitchels--Mary E Elis   43

June 13, 1871   William H Delane-- Emma H Donaldson   46

July 4, 1871   Heinrich Pape--Sophia Pfortner   53
      [groom of St Louis bride of Pilot Knob]
July 9, 1871   William H Kinney--Rebecca M Ward   112

June 24 1871   George Patrick--Mary Reeves   71

July 4, 1871   George R Hartsock--Mary E York   52

July 27 1871   Joseph Kelerson?--Mary Boska   45

May 6, 1871   Byrd Pryor--Polly Sarena Crocker   37

July 23, 1871   Henry J. Boothby--Lizzie A Risser   99

May 8, 1871   James Acorn-- Zenia Smith   37

July 9, 1871   James Parker--Mary Ellen Reese   50

Aug 21, 1871   John W Sutton--Artimesia Dunn   46

May 14 1871   John Thurman--Sarah Jane Hatridge   129

April 10, 1870?   Harrison Denin--Nancy Jane Buckner   151

July 13 1871   John A Pressly--Margaret P Howard   81

July 25, 1871   Irvin Rea--Mrs Margaret J Ringold   17

Date	Names	Page
Nov 7, 1871	Samuel Hull--Octavia W Taylor	81
	[groom of Wash Co ·bride of Iron Co]	
Aug 13, 1871	John D Lambird--Jarush Ann Johnston	115
Aug 31, 1871	Moritz Weise--Mathilda Huck	45
Sept 31, 1871	W R Roberts--Sarah Jane Kinard	45
Sept. 23, 1871	Lawrenze Reinhard--Pauline Gegg	135
	[Now of Fenburg, Ste Genevieve Co Mo]	
Oct 26, 1871	Daniel M C. Smith--Frances E Belman	103
Oct 12, 1871	William Sizemore--Melissa M Casteel	12
Sept. 17, 1871	Joseph E. Smith--Mary J Vandigrif	128
Aug 6 . 1871	Henry Vandigrift--Mary Melvina Rial	128
Aug 20 1871	R O Edward--Narcissa E Waters	128
Aug 25, 1871	William G. Wadlow--Elizabeth J Allcorn	121
Oct 20, 1871	Herman Wesche-- Juliane Will	53
Nov 15, 1871	Henry J Webb--Joanah H Farr	161
Nov 14, 1871	Heinrich Dreyer--Margaret Mortimer	53
Oct 15, 1871	Joseph Jenkins --Mahala A Vicery	39
Nov 14, 1871	Joseph P McNail--Mary A Shrieve	26
Nov 3, 1871	William W Reyburn--Elizabeth J Russell	13
Nov 22, 1871	W E Trapp--Mary A Boatright	71
Dec 3, 1871	Elias K Callihan--Nancy Walker	91
Oct 3. 1871	John Akers--Milly Thompson	110
Feb 10, 1871	James Ruble--Margaret Marlow	35
Sept 25 1871	C W Tally--Nancy Ann Stidham	35
Oct 5. 1871	Green Marberry --Nancy J Inman	77
Dec 12, 1871	John W Galestin--Julia Reel	52
Dec 25, 1871	William T Gay--Lucy Catherine Logan	134
Dec 27, 1871	James W Hogan--Susan Brown	46
Dec 31, 1871	Howell Loyd--Margaret D Horton	71

Dec 27, 1871   William Anderson--Parlee Hanks   71

Jan 1 1872   Mitchell McFadden--Hannah Waldon   45
                 [both colored]
Jan 6 1871   Thomas Murphy--Mary Ward   112

Oct 15, 1871   Joseph Ruble--Amanda Hickman   112

Oct 19, 1871   Samuel P Hampton--Eliza Oharron   134

Jan 10, 1872   Frederick R Bryant--Annie M Purkiss   134

Jan 10 1872   Robert E Purkiss--Lizzie J Logan   134

Dec 21, 1871   A J Puls--Anne L Behrens   20

Jan 10 1872   A M Cline --Abigail Edmonds   20

Nov 14, 1871   H B Pease--Augusta Beckwick   79

--   -- ----   John L Crow--Jenney Yancey   79
            [filed Feb 3, 1872
Oct -- 1871   John Ruble --Angeline Kelison   35
            [" on the 5th Sunday in Oct 1871
Jan 13, 1872   Thomas Fleming--Martha Gross   151

Feb 18, 1872   John Stewart--Sarah Jane Henderson   151

Jan 11, 1872   Paten Martin --Lizzie Kelly   52

Jan 31, 1872   George W Adams--Charlotte L Henderson   --

Dec 17 1871   Robert Davidson--Margaret Eldrich   112

Feb 14, 1872   William Jones --Carzenia Dickson   152

Feb 29 1872   James Thompson--Betcy Mansel   37
            [" joined in holey Mallry Money"]

Jan 21 1872   David L Woodward--Emily J Charlton   126

Mar 4, 1872   Chas R Boaz--Margaret Annie Kassinger   45

Jan 20 1872   Andrew Sullivan--Mrs Josephine Nelson   110

Mar 11, 1872   Jacob Hutmacher--Coprenia Burger   45

Mar 3, 1872   John W Duty--Mary L Wood   3

April 11 1872   N M Anderson--Susanah Hudlston   19

April 14 1872   Paul Dinwiddy--Amanda Shelton   142

May 14 1871   Philip Kolb--Emilie Kolb   45

Feb 13, 1872   Bowlin Farr--Sarah E Layman   17

April 4 1872   Alexander Brooks--Angeline Latham   154
         [groom of" Renals County"]

Mar 21 1872   J M Roope--Alvira Douglass   20

April 9, 1872   Herman Jacobson--Mary Hitzeman   20

May 25, 1872   John Millican--Elizabeth King   20

May 26, 1872   Henry W Baker--Martha Nebergall   71
         [groom of Reynolds Co .bride of Iron Co.]
June 5, 1872   Frank Johnson--Hardenia Marcum   71
         [groom of Springfield, Il , bride of Iron Co]
May 9, 1872   Modast Rapp--Malinda Weaver   77

June 9, 1872   Jackson Walsh--Elizabeth J Keltner   17
     [both of the city of St Louis]
July 3, 1872   John W Henson --Hannah Belle Weaver   77

July 5, 1872   Stephen C Wright--Mary J McCarrey   45

July 21, 1872   Taylor Nickless--Tennessee Casteel   45

July 25, 1872   Henry Rashe--Anna Margaretha Mickel   45

July 13 1872   Solomon Jones--Margaret Stevenson   50

May 12, 1872   Elvis M Hodgg--Amanda L Flinn   31

Aug 23, 1872   James J Cuddy--Kate Murphy   17

June 25, 1872   Jasper Goddard--Lucy A Harwick   164

Sept 1, 1872   Thomas Smith-- Elizabeth C Ball   25

Sept 8, 1872   James Henry Sutton--Eliza Jane Smith   45

Nov 9 1871?   John Alcorn--Ambie Angeline Rowel   1

Sept 23, 1872   Martin Vandergrift--Alridy White   45

April 10 1867? William Levin- Sarah Jane Tong   17

Aug 15, 1872   F C Townsend--Mary E Wiatt   143

Oct 3 1872   Alexander Bird--Mary Ann Quisenberry   143

Aug 7, 1872   Westly Faulkner --Eliza Jane Ramsey   115

Oct. 24 1872   Victor Meslen--Louisa Johnson   71

Iron County Marriages
Book " A " 1857-1873

Oct	27, 1872	William Simpson-- Minerva J Dennis	45
Oct	31 1872	Soloman Sax--Celia Ann Reed	42
Oct	7. 1866?	Jacob Moyer--Arminta Highley	78
Nov	12, 1872	Christopher Newberry--Elizabeth Lane	111
Nov	25. 1872	James C Davis --Jennie Wall	126
Oct	1, 1972	Isaac Stokely--Mary C O'Neal	31
Oct	12, 1872	John Singer--Harriet Burck	60
Nov	25, 1872	James Henry Clarke--Mary Whitworth	17

[groom of St Francois Co ,bride of Iron Co   ]

Dec	11, 1872	Robert C Parks-- Eliza George	71
Dec	17. 1872	Thomas J Hampton--Emmeline Gowen	71
Nov	16, 1872	Joseph Brewer--Martha Ratliff	71
Dec	25. 1872	Foster Duty-- Lucinda Pentacraft	3
Dec	5, 1872	Peter Pawley--Lucinda Hawk	4
Oct	10, 1872	John Reily--Lucy Jane Slone	--
Jan	1, 1873	Joseph F Lindsay--Emilie A Russell	17
Jan	13 1873	John H Johnson--Ruth Lowe	71
Jan	26, 1873	Henry Orrick-- Susan C Sutton	71
Feb	2 1873	James Hasty--Lucy Shrum	45
Dec	12. 1872	Landers T Ramsy--Martha J Howel	115
Feb	8 1873	Thomas Kennon--Ellen Beckett	1
Jan	26. 1873	Franklin DuChien--Mary E Graham	71
Feb	25. 1873	James Brown--Julia Ann Rasnick	45
Nov	5, 1873	George Willis--Sarah Morgan	127
Jan	28 1873	Frank Layton--Emily Meisenheimer	127
Feb	9, 1873	G W Lashley--Rachael Jane Brewer	1
April 16	1863?	Ecide Snerer-- Christine Schaefer	45
Aug	7, 1870?	James A Hautz--Elizabeth Crump	45

40

Iron County Marriages
Book " A " 1857-1873

Sept 30, 1870 Jacob Halterman—-Sophia Hall   45

Nov 15, 1873? John Bosswell- - Elizabeth Jane Roberson 45

Names of Ministers or Justices who Performed marriages in Book " A

1	Lewis Abrams , MG Bapt	41	T D Davis, MG
2	David Adams, MG	42	Jabez H Hennman, MG ME
3	John R Adams. Mg	43	Thomas J Dickerson, MEP
4	Nelson Adams, MG	44	Joseph Dines, MG MES
5.	Zenas Adams MG	45	Franz Dinger, JP
6	J T Ake, JP	46	John Donaldson, MG Presby
7	William Allcorn, JP	47	Samuel H. H Huff, MG ME
8	B. O Allen, MG Bapt	48.	Wm. C Edington , Xian Ch
9	L. F Aspley, MG Mes	49	Geo. M Effinger --
10	James C. Asher, MG	50	Bowlin Farr, MG
11	T. G Atchison, MG Mes	51	W.J Ferrell
12	James F. Baker, MG	52	John W. Finley, MG
13	Thomas C Barrett MG Presby	53	Herm Flacksbart, MG
14	Ph Barth, MG	54	E R Fort --
15	George P Beard. MG	55	John Gardner, MG
16	John F Bennger, MG Luth	56	William P Gibson MG MES
17.	Jerome C Berryman MG Mes	57	Chas Groeber, MG Luth
18	Samuel Black, MG	58	Wm D Hamilton, MG Bapt
19.	John W Boggs MG	59	J W Hancock, JP
20	A D Boss, JP	60	Jacob Hartzell, JP
21	John Bounds JP	61	A H Heinlein MG
22	G F Brooks, MG ME	62	A W Henderson , 13th IL CA|
23	J. G Butler, MG	63	John J Hennessey, MG
24	John W Call, JP	64	William Henson, MG
25	Johnson M Carle MG	65	G W Hull, MG
26	J M Carter, Bapt	66	P H Jaqueth MG
27	A M Casteel JP	67	James C Johnson, JP
28	Erin Chrisco, MG Mes	68	Nathan Johnson, MG
29	Eleazer G Clay, JP	69	Jefferson Johnston, Bapt.
30	E H Clayton, JP	70	James Kendall, MG
31	W H Cook MG	71	J B Kinney, JP
32	Issac Copeland, MG	72	A Kleinegers, MG
33	James Copeland MG	73	A W Kness, JP
34	William Crafford, MG	74	Charles Kobler, MG Luth
35	John Crowley MG	75	Isaac Lane, MG
36	Joseph Crawley, MG	76	Philip Lankford, Cum 38
37	William T Crocker MG	77	Amos V Lashley, MG Bap
38	George C Crow MG	78	D M Lee, MG
39	J. B. Daniel --?	79	L M Lewis. MG MES
40	Thomas J Davidson, MG	80	John V Logan, JP

81 H M Long, MG Mes
82 William C Love JP
83 C H Lovejoy, 7th Ks Cav
84 A G Lucas MG
85 Samuel Lucass, JP
86 R R. McCoy, 3rd Mo Cav
87 Peter McCracken, MG
88 B S McNail MG
89 William H Maddox, MG
90 Isaac Martin, Chris Church
91 John Martin, MG
92 Robert C Martin MG
93 Joshua Mason, JP
94 A A Mathes, MG
95 Edwin May, JP
96 Henry Mears, ?
97 Geo H W Miller, P
98 Jacob Miller MG
99 John Monteeth, ?
100 William J Murray, MG
101 Lewis Rrick, MG Bapt.
102 Harvey Palmer, JP
103 Andrew Peace, MG MES
104. C R Peek JP
105 William A Pogue, MG
106 William Polk, MG
107 Alfred H Powell, MG
108 Jesse R Pratt, Bapt
109 Matthew Y Pratt, B
110 Wm Quisenberry JP
111 James Rayney, Jp
112 Ira Rayney, JP
113 John G Rauft, JP
114 Absolem Reau, MG
115 Robert A Rich, MG
116 Sidney Richmond MG
117 Levi Rowland, MG
118 L F Rowland MG
119 Theodore P Russell, JP
120 S G Rutter --
121 Robert Seal, MG
122 Callaway Seizemore JP
123 George S Sellers, JP
124 William W Settle, MG
125 David W Shaver, JP
126 William M Shelton MG
127 William O Short, MG
128 Simeon G Shuler JP
129 J T Shrum, MG
130 H Side MG ME

131 Thomas C Smith, MG Presby
132 Porter H Snow, MG
133 Hiram L Speir, JP
134 Julis Spencer, MG
135. T T STein, --
136 George W Stephens, JP
137 John Strickland, Bapt
138. William Suits, JP
139 J R Tamblyn, MG
140 John F Taylor, JP
141 C Tays MG
142 Henry Thomas, MG
143 John Thomas, Mg Mes
144 Horace F Tong, --
145 Lewis Tucker, Cath P
146 Magness Tullock, --
147 Samuel Tullock, JP
148 Walter B Trumbull, MG Mes
149 Hugh Twomy, parson
150 Andrew J Vance, Bapt
151 James H Vail, Judge Cir
152 Andrew Wallis, Mg
153 Jesse B Wallis , MG
154 John Webb, MG
155 E H White, MG
156 William White JP
157 Henry Whitnah, JP
158 Joseph H Whitnah, JP
159 E D Wilkins, 21stReg IL
160 ------Williams JP
161 John C Williams, MG
162 W M Williams MG
163 D A Wilson, MG Presby.
164 James C Wilson, JP
165 G C Wingo, JP
166 W S Woodard, MG

Iron County Marriages
Book " A " 1857-1873

This is an index for Book " A " only Both books will have their ov
index
A
Abrams 41
Absher 12
Acorn 36
Adair 12
Adams 3,10,11,12,21,28,31,34,
38,41
Agairs 12
Ahreis 21
Ailer 1
Ake 2,6,22,28,32,41
Akers 36,37
Albridge 22
Albright 32
Aldright 7
Alcorn 6, 16 20,37,39,41
Aley 15
Allcock 18
Allen 41
Alley 12
Allison 20
Allridge 20
Amett 4,8
Ammons 4
Amoldy 27
Anderson 14,20 26.32,38
Andis 35
Andress 28
Andrews 21,31
Ann 18
Anthony 25
Appel 25
Antis 74
Armes 18
Arnett 10,23,33
Arisman 33
Armstrong 20
Arnold 9,15,20 28
Arthur 1
Asbury 31
Ashberry 12
Asher 3 20,41
Ashlock 22
Aspley 41
Asterbrook 14
Atchison 5.41
Aubuchon 34
Ausdon 15
Austin 28
B
Baker 4 12 34,39 41
Bailey 33

Baird 3
Bales 12
Ballard 3
Ball 39
Ballew 14
Banes 23
Barbett 25
Banks 19
Barbut 20
Barger 25,30,38
Barree 13
Barrett 41
Barrow 35
Barsche 26
Barth 41
Bartlebaugh 27
Barthelow 1
Barton 24
Bartley 28
Bates 24
Baughman 5
Baxter 14
Beachman 33
Beal 3,35
Beard 30 41
Beck 8 12
Beckett 22 40
Beckley 2
Beckman 24 29
Beckwick 38
Beeman 33
Behrens 38
Bell 4,11, 13,14,29,32,33
Belman 37
Belmar 18
Bennger 41
Berch 31 33
Bergman 31
Berner 18
Berrington 18
Berryman 14 19 22 24 41
Bershur 33
Birch 7
Bird 39
Bishop 35
Black 11,41
Bland 8
Boargouis 31
Boatwright 36 37
Boaz 38
Boel 13

B
Boggs 6,26,41
Bolinger 25
Bollinger 21 27 30,36
Bollock 15
Bone 1,3,7,22
Bonney 16
Boos 16
Boothby 36
Boothe 8
Boren 10
Boss 5,9,12
Bosworth 12
Boswell 6,10,12,32
Bounce 34
Bounds 41
Bourgin 30
Boyd 26
Bowlin 13
Bradberry 22
Bradshaw 12,28
Brady 36
Braeur 21
Brannum 5
Breaton 25
Breitenatein 25
Brewer 2 4 8,9,35 40
Brewington 16,17
Brickey 18
Brill 4,28,29
Brimingham 25
Britenbaker 6
Britten 11
Brock 10,11 17,22
Brogean 36
Boska 36
Brook 9,10,13,36,39,41
Brown 4,7 10 14,20 28,36 37 40
Bruce 23
Bruer 4,34
Brouner 13
Bryan 10,15,36
Bryant 18 36
Buck 27
Buckner 5 21 28 36
Buford 20
Buggs 2 21
Burns 10
Burnyard 19
Burch 19
Burden 22
Burgan 34
Burk 6 27 40
Burnett 26

Butler
Burt 18
Bush 2
Bushew 12
Byrd 1
C
Cain 23
Caldwell 21
Calihan 5,32,34
Call 41
Callaway 1
Callihan 37
Callison 9
Camel 30
Campbell 26,28,29 31 33 35
Canaday 33
Carahan 9,11
Carder 12
Carl 34
Carle 41
Carlton 24
Carmack 4
Carmichal 10
Carpenter 8
Carter 3,12,21,22,28,33,39
Caseboult 24
Caserly 12
Casey 28
Cassaday 31
Casteel 2 3 4 7,9,37 39,41
Cauldwell 19
Cayce 32
Craven 22
Cenceboy 9
Chapman 15 21
Champers 17
Chandlers 25
Chappel 28
Charlton 38
Chauvin 5
Child 9
Childers 25
Chilton 2,4,20,25 34
Choice 18
Clapper 2 19
Clark 8 32 40
Clary 30
Clay 10 41
Claybaugh 23
Clayton 28,41
Clemmons 30
Cline 24 25 38
Close 35

Club 36
Cochman 35
Cofman 33
Coldwell 28,30
Cole 9,10,28,36
Coleman 30
Collier 22
Collins 4 7 15 17,29 33
Colston 29
Compton 5,20 35
Conley 23
Conway 28
Cooley 18
Cook 13,41
Cooper 26,34
Copeland 16 25,41
Cora 34
Corder 31
Cotrell 13
Counts 5 20
Cowan 13,22
Cox 21 23 28
Crain 13
Crafford 41
Craven 22
Creath 24 31 34
Creth 9 24
Crico 26
Crisco 14 41
Crocker 10,19,36.41
Croley 17
Crossgrove 11
Crosshan 22
Crow 24,28,41
Crowford 17
Crowley 10,41
Crownover 25
Crump 39
Cuddy 39
Cuning 19
Cunningham 36
Cuddy 39
        D
Daire 15
Dale 17
Danels 24
Daniels 14,41
Danley 35
Daroney 17
Davidson 8 12 15 19,28 33 38 41
Davis 8 19,20 35,40,41
Day 4 19
Dean 9 13,26
Dearmint 31

Death 25
Delano 29
Delts 29
Denby 10
Denin 36
Dennis 7,33,40
Dennison 18
Denny 25
Dequire 31
Derrick 31
Derry 35
Detherew 21
Detheron 28
Dettman 25 27
Dettmer 9,24
Dickard 33
Dickens 20 23
Dickerson 9,41
Dickson 25,35,36,38
Dienst 30
Diggs 31
Dill 29
Dilts 31
Dines 10,41
Dinger 4,41
Dinwiddy 38
Donaldson 29 41
Donally 19
Donoho 2
Donohue 21
Doshea 18
Dougan 22
Douglass 20,39
Doughtrty 17,18
Doyle 26
Drachter 3
Dreyer 37
Duchien 40
Dudley 25,26
Dugan 7
Dunegan 6
Dusenberry 11
Duty 20 38 40
        E
Eaden 14
Eddington 5
Edgar 12
Edington 20,41
Edison 20,36
Edmiston10
Edmonds 4 7 9 16 38
Edmmunds 28
Edmons 30
Edwards 11,21 37

Effinger 41
Elders 22
Eldrich 38
Elliot 21,27
Ellis 13 19,21 36
Ellit 18
Elser 24
Emboden 20
Emmons 26
Engleman 11
Engel 15 26
Epler 14
Erden 14
Ernst 9
Essenwien 30,34
Ethington 18
Evans 15,21,26,32,34
Ezell 12
   F
Fagan 33,34
Fairbrother 17
Fairchild 29,31
Fairene 5
Fake 16
Farmer 5,7 29
Farr 27 37,39 41
Farrar 6 21 33
Farris 33
Fass 21
Fasterling 9
Faught 8
Faulkenberry 25
Faulkner 39
Fax 18
Ferguson 18 24 27
Ferrel 4 8 41
Ferrier 18
Filley 17
Finley 41
Fitzpatrick 1,16,21
Fleeman 33
Fleming 38
Flinn 39
Flowers 16,18 22,27
Flourz 32
Fogs 19
Folabinbe 17
Foister 26
Fooks 6 27
Forehand 32
Forgerson 10
Forster 21
Fortener 6

Foster 28
Fowler 15
Franks 2 19
Frame 10
Francis 6
Frazier 7
Freeman 17
Frett 11
Friar 22
Frissell 14
Fritzwater 12
   G
Gaedart 3
Gainter 14
Galestin 37
Gardner 41
Garrett 31
Gaston 27
Gay 29,37
Gegg 37
Gemerson 26
Gentry 16
George 15,29,31,33,40
Gibson 2,12,10,20,24,26,34,41
Gideon 23
Gilbert 5
Gilliam 29
Goddard 26,39
Goggin 14,27
Gollerhugh 21
Goodman 5 16
Goodwin 22
Gore 6
Gowen 40
Graham 40
Gragg 2,5 6,9
Grandhomme 12,32
Granky 12
Grass 28
Gray 6
Grayum 28
Green 4,6,10 16,18,34,35
Grigsby 22 29,31
Grill 13
Grimes 17 18
Groeber 41
Gross 38
Groves 11 19,22,25 31
Guffey 22 32
Guinin 17 18
Gunner 1
Gunnett 25
Gulivar 8 27
Guyto 21

H

Haan 3
Hall 1,8 9,10,11 17 26,30
Hale 23
Haller 30
Handcock 41
Hampton 1 16,29,38,40
Hamilton 41
Handcock 24,27
Hanks 34 38
Hannah 8
Harbison 2,4 34
Hardwick 39
Hardridge 5 10
Harlan 5
Harman 11
Harper 35
Harris 56 8 19,23,31,32
Harrison 24,32,33
Hartgrove 9 23,32
Hartman 28
Hartsock 36
Hartzell 25,41
Harvey 29
Hasty 16,20,21,28,40
Hatridge 36
Hautz 40
Hawk 24 40
Hawkins 24
Haunapple 13
Haynes 7
Haywood 23
Head 12,20
Healy 19
Hearing 15
Heckleman 30
Heinricks 9,25
Helms 26
Helton 32
Henderson 8 13 30 38 41
Hendrick 15
Hennessey 41
Henry 5
Henson 3,4,8,20 28 39 41
Herald 27
Heuring 15
Hews 11
Hickeritz 26
Hickman 4 10,27 38
Hicks 14
Heinricks 9
Higden 21
Highley 9,32,34,35 40
Hilderbrand 34 35

Hill 10,26
Hinchey 1
Hine 31
Hitzerman 39
Hodgg 39
Hofmeister 26
Hogan 5 37
Hohanstricet 13
Hollats 11
Hollatz 12
Hollman 1,5 32
Holt 24
Holly 18
Hood 34
Honey 12
Horn 17
Horton 2,5,13 16,27,29,35 37
House 31
Hovy 30
Howard 3,8,13,24,36
Howell 15,17,40
Howington 18
Hoy 11
Hubble 31
Hubel 5
Huck 37
Hudleston 25 38
Hues 24
Huff 1,3,7,24,26,27,30,32 34,35
Hughes 4,27
Hughs 15
Hull 37,41
Humole
Hunt 19,20,23
Hunter 11
Hurts 12,21 26
Huston 14
Hutchens 17,34
Hutmacher 38
Hutzeman 39
Hyden 35

I

Imboden 1 6 8,9 10 22
Ingle 1
Ingram 19
Inman 1,2 4,7,9 13 31 37
Irvan 31
Irvin 33
Ivester 11
Ivis 33

J

Jackman 10
Jackson 2 27,28 29

Jacobson 39
James 33
Jaquesth 41
Javes 36
Jenkins 37
Johns 21
Joiner 14,15 16
Jointer 16,25
Johnson 2,4,10 11,20 26 27 29,30
34,39,40,41
Johnston 8,37
Joice 1
Jones 3 4 7 11 17 18 19 27,31 35
38,39
Jorden 2,32
Jorris 27
Justice 26
K
Kaesenhagen 14
Kaffer 20
Kassemacher 33
Kassinger 38
Kaths 16
Kauffman 29
Keach 35
Kearnes 27
Kearney
Keath 25
Keathley 31
Keffer 14
Kelerson 36
Kelison 17,36
Kelly 17,21,22,24,27 38
Keltner 20 39
Kemble 25
Kemp 1
Kendall 41
Kenner 22
Kenney 17,36
Kennon 40
Ketcherside 1 3 25
Ketcheson 33
Kims 15
Kinard 37
Kinekel 27
King 15 29 39
Kinkcad 29
Kinkland 28 32
Kinney 41
Kirk 5 35
Kitchell 20,36
Kleineger 41
Kleinigus 30

Knapp 5
Knees 21 41
Knit 32
Kobler 41
Kohlhage 17,24
Kolb 10,11 24,26,27,38
L
Labrash 11
Lackey 12
Lagraint 15
Laine 7
Lakey 31
Lambird 37
Lammsback 9
Landabauch 7
Lando 35
Lane 6,22,40,41
Langford 41
Lankiston 35
Lashley 5,18,21,22 26 34 40 41
Latham 15,27,39
Layman 39
Layton 40
Leadbetter 8
Lee 7,20,27,28,41
Legat 6
Legbetter 11
Leggett 11
Legrand 29 31
Leonard 5,18
Lerke 7
Lester 33
Levin 39
Lewis 2,3,6,25,30,34 41
Liles 5
Linch 15
Lindsay 4,26,40
Linz 11
Literal 3
Litrel 25
Livingstone 9,12
Lloyd 2,19
Loid 22 23
Logan 2 3 9 37 38 41
Long 33,42
Louis 10
Love 13 14 35 42
Lovejoy 41
Lowe 40
Loyd 5,6 30,37
Lucus 17,42
Ludy 32
Lukes 15

Luthy 28
Lyman 35
M
McAlister 11
McCabe 17
McCalister 9
McCallum 27
McClanahan 8
McCarrey 39
McCracken 42
McColough 23
McColley 30
McCollum 4
McCoy 42
McDaniel 32
McDowell 8,13
McFadden 4,19,20,21,22,38
McFarland 23
McFerson 8
McGarnigan 26
McGregory 13
McKinney 12,31
McMain 8
McLaferity 7
McLain 33
McMurtry 6
McMurty 23
McNail 25,31,32 37 41
McNeely 4,9
Mackland 17
Maddox 42
Madkins 23,33
Mahan 18
Mairten 23
Mangel 29
Mansel 38
Mark 16
Marlow 7,29,37
Mason 1 21,34,42
Martin 10,19,20,,23,25,26,29,32,33,
34,38 42
Mathes 42
Matthew 2 21
Marler 27
Matenev 33
May 42
Mayberry 5 6 8 17 31 32
Mayfield 24,33
Mayo 4 16
Mead 25
Mears 42
Meders 26
Meisenheimer 40
Menger 11

Merricks 20
Merrill 22 24 30
Meslen 39
Messer 3,9,20 32
Meyers 6
Michel 39
Middleton 8
Miland 33
Milburn 8
Miller 4,5,9 10 19,25 26,27,
31,32 33,35,42
Millican 39
Mills 3,14,16,32
Millsap 13
Mires 12,18,21
Mitchell 9,16
Moerkel 30
Moody 13
Moore 5 6,7,19,23 25,29
Mond 16,17
Montgomery 24
Monteeth 42
Morgan 5,6,15,25,27 28 29,40
Morris 2,17,34
Mortimer 37
Morton 8,9
Moser 28 29
Moses 6
Moss 1
Mouser 16
Moyer 20 42
Muffey 9
Munz 16
Murphy 38,39
Murray 10,20,42
Muse 25
Murphy 38,39
Myres 33
Napier 1,25
Nalle 22,24
Nealy 20
Nearren 13
Nebergall 39
Neely 9,17
Neighbors 24
Neill 25
Nelson 38
Newberry 2,21,30,40
Newman 29 30
Newton 3,36
Nicholas 25
Nichols 10 26
Nickless 39
Nix 32

Norman 6
Norris 1 25
Norton 19
  O
O'Bannon 18,26 32
Oden 13
Odonnell 18,25
Odom 9
Oehler 14
Oen 23
Oharron 38
Olney 14
O'Neader 31

O'Neil 31,34,40
Orie 25
Ormes 27
Orrick 2,4,6,40
Osburn 17
Othman 30
Owen 1

  P
Palmer 1,38,9,25,30,33,42
Palmore 6
Park 7,40
Parker 1 5 15 17,32 36
Parman 11
Parmer 15 18
Parson 8
Patrick 36
Patterson 2
Paulas 29
Pawley 40
Pearson 7 35
Pease 1,2,27,28,34,38,42
Peck 4,5,19,29,30 35
Peek 42
Peel 24
Peetz 28,29
Pence 11
Pentacraft 40
Perigan 14
Perry 24
Pershkey 6
Peter 9
Petty 1,6 33
Phillips 21,25,31 32
Piece 14
Pierson 7
Piles 23
Pinkney 1,13 _4,30
Pitman 27
Pits 3

Pogue 42
Polk 6,31,42
Pollard 32
Polley 28
Polless 6
Posten 13,17
Potter 5,17
Powell 42
Pratt 7,42
Priest 17
Proffit 25
Prough 2 6,22,24
Pryor 36
Pullam 15,32
Puls 38
Purkiss 38
  Q
Quinton 15,16
Quisenberry 2 9,39,42
  R
Radach 33
Ragan 13
Rahm 24,28
Raines 18
Ramsey 7,13,39,40
Randels 32
Raney 23
Rapp 39
Rashe 39
Rasnick 40
Rategan 33
Ratliff 10,17,40
Rauft 27 28,32 42
Rawlinghs 28
Rayfield 13
Rayney 42
Rea 36
Read 20,42
Reaves 13
Rechert 29
Redding 17
Reed 2,3,4,11,20,23 40
Reeder 13
Reek 23
Reel 25 37
Reeves 3 25 26
Reid 14
Reily 40
Reinhard 37
Reneau 2
Renfro 3
Renicks 8
Resin 7
Reubottom 24

Reven 13
Reves 29
Revis 27
Reyburn 1,14,16 23,31,37
Rhyme 6
Rice 25,52
Rich 3,42
Richards 2
Richardson 6,15,27
Richeson 33
Richman 3,23,42
Rial 37
Ridanny 30
Richter 14 23
Riddle 28
Ridgely 12
Ringer 8,12
Ringold 36
Risser 36
Rivers 25
Robbins 12
Robbs 7.11 14,.22,27
Roberts 16,34,37
Robertson 13
Robinson 2
Robison 25
Robitt 18
Rodes 15
Roe 3,8
Roeslein 12 28
Rohdes 29
Romer 16
Roods 1
Roop 27 29
Roope 39
Rose 4 10 25
Ross 13,16
Roth 30
Rothen 9
Rouse 1 2,3
Row 2
Rowel 39
Rowland 42
Rrick 42
Rubel 24,30,35,38
Rucker 25
Ruebottom 19
Rupe 11
Rutledge 8
Rutschman 35
Rutter 42
Ryan 30 35
  S
Sahr 3

Salsberry 13
Sample 20
Sanders 5,15.30
Sandford 5
Satterfield 24
Savage 1,8
Sax 40
Scagg 29
Scarbrough 27
Scherrenbeck 7
Schiefer 13
Schmith 15
Schmitz 11,22,28
Schneider 32
Schoen 26
Scholer 5
Schreckenbert 30
Schwab 1,17
Scruitchfield 20
Scrogins 30
Seabert 2
Seal 21,23,26,30
Segmore 7
Seigman 34
Seile 24
Seitz 1,19
Sellers 42
Seltser 33
Sensaboy 6
Sergert 5
Settle 42
Shanon 18
Shaeffer 23,40
Shafer 11
Shaffner 14
Sharp 14
Shaver 16,42
Shearer 4,10,40
Shell 6
Shelton 1,5,30.38 42
Shepard 1
Sherelds 6
Shorer 35
Sherill 12,28
Short 42
Shouf 12
Snrieve 37
Shrrum 14,42
Shrum 2 14 25 28,40
Shullz 23
Shwlar 4 42
Sides 24
Sidge 17
Sights 18

Simpson 40
Sims 5
Sinclair 4,28 31
Singer 40
Singleton 4
Sipe 42
Site 11
Silvey 10
Sizemore 22 37 42
Skiner 18
Sladeck 14
Sloan 9,13 27 30,33
Slone 12,15 24 40
Slos 5,18
Smith 1,2 3 5,6 7 9 10,11 12,13
14,16,18 19,21,23 30,32,33,34,35
36,37 39
Smyth 33
Snow 5,28 42
Snyder 23,27
Sorpherra 19
Sowers 9
Spangler 31,34,35
Sparge 30
Speck 13
Spencer 8,19 42
Spier 7 42
Spragly 31
Stanton 35
Statler 32
Steel 20
Stegall 12
Stein 42
Steine 1
Stephenson 34
Stephens 2,7,11,22,24,42
Stevenson 16 31 34,39
Stevens 13,19,22,24
Stewart 8 9,38
Stidham 31
StJohn 27
Stokley 40
Strickland 8 16 18,42
Strumbaugh 35
Stubes 2
Sturm 15
Suits 42
Sullivan 27 28
Sumpter 13 14,24
Sutterfield 27
Sutton 1 4 7 8 26 28 29 35 36 39 40
Swadley 35
Swearengin 4 11 22
Sweeny 20 28

Sweny 18
Symps 11
T
Tamblyn 42
Tally 37
Taylor 2,3,4,6 9,16 24 26,30
34,36 37 42
Tays 42
Tedder 7
Temme 27
Terly 32 34
Terrell 2 31
Tetley 4,8
Thacker 12
Theil 33
Therman 26
Thomas 9,11,12,20,21,23,29,33,
35,42
Thomason 10,36
Thomasson 24
Thompson 4 5 6 10,17 18,20,21,
22,23,25,26,29,36,37,38
Thurman 10,36
Tierney 25
Timmons 25
Timlin 35
Tilley 30
Tobin 12
Tong 31 39,42
Toothe 15
Tournbaugh 13,14
Towsend 39
Trapp 37
Treace 33
Trollinger 13 14
Trow 5
Trumbull 42
Tual 11
Tubbs 16
Tucker 2 42
Tullock 3,10 23 26 32,42
Turnbow 24
Turner 11 14 15 23 26
Twomy 42
Tyrell 28 32
U
Underwood 9
Usrey 33
V
Vail 42
Valle 18
Valley 29 32
Vallie 16
Vance 1 2 42

Vandigrift 37,39
Vants 7
Vasterling 21
Vaughn 14 17,34
Vest 15,23
Viceery 37
Vickmarm 10
Vickory 17 22
    W
Waddell 16
Wadlow 37
Walden 18,24,26,38
Walker 21 28,35 57
Wall 33,40
Wallace 16,17,23
Wallis 3,22,31,34,35,42
Walsh 39
Ward 26,36,38
Warner 10,23
Warsham 28
Warsing 2,6,23,29
Warren 18,35
Waters 19,37
Watson 3,4,9
Watts 13
Weaver 39
Webb 9,11,16 25,26,33 42
Weber 15
Weble 34
Webster 22
Weise 4,12,37
Weitt 14
Wesche 37
Wessenstein 8
West 16
Westeney 9
Westerman 9
Westfall 33
Wezeners 3
Whaler 25
Whit 12
White 1,19,23,28,39,42
Whitener 22,26
Whitner 21
Whittmore 11
Whitnah 42
Whitworth 31 40
Wiatt 39
Wiley 2
Wilkins 42
Will 29 37
Willett 36
Willford 9
Williamson 25

Williams 3,4,5 8,13 15,19 20
22 25 26 27,28
Willis 8,40
Wimon 15
Wimpy 19
Wilson 6,11,12 16 18,19,23,
35,42
Wingo 42
Winn 3,34
Wood 14,15,20,21,26,28
Woodard 42
Woodward 38
Woolem 32
Wright 12,36,39
Wyatt 21,22
Wyatte 29
    X
    Y
Yancey 38
Yancy 2
Yankey 34
Yater 36
York 36
Young 3 10 12 15,20,26
    Z
Zimmerman 3,23
Zink 5
Zuber 11
Zute 21
Names over looked
in Index
Skiles 22
Longgreat 22
Millener 22
Pfeil 22
Pfortner 36
Pape 36

Iron County, Missouri Marriages
Book B 1873-1881

DATE	NAME	Min or J P
Sept 5 1872	Andrew Wallis--Nancy E King	89
Feb 9 1873	John Reeves--Mary E Joines	89
Dec 17, 1871?	Robert Davison--Margaret Eldridge	89
Nov 3 1872?	Jesse J Harrison--Abby Sheets	89
Oct 28, 1872	Peter Ruble--Alice A Gowen	114
Nov 14 1872	Henry Caldwell--Minnie Merrill	90
Mar 23, 1873	Jasper Graham--Hanah Bailey	112
Feb 17 1873	John Smith-- Irene Canada	73
Mar 13, 1873	Gallenous S Petty--Rebecca Jane Jones	73
April 10, 1873	Samuel Bond--Sarah Quisenberry	73
April 22, 1872?	John knight--Celia Roberts	106
April 24 1873	Michael Huck--Regina Neuberger	33
	[wit C K Miller 7 H W Delano]	
April 26 1873	Andrew Patrick--Lucinda E Snort	66
April 27, 1873	Francis Webb--Mattie Warren	66
April 12 1873	John Thomas Chandler--Mary Morgan	29
April 20, 1873	Burges Lick--Bethena Reeves	29
April 30 1873	F R Raney--Jane Rease	29
April 6, 1873	Lavega Self--Marcia Jane Huff	1
May 6 1873	Harrison Dearing--Sarah Jane Stewart	33
May 15 1873	William H Winfield--Lillian Tong	64
	[groom of Little Rock Ark bride of Ironton]	
May 11 1873	John Clements--Susan A Hall	105
June 15, 1873	John H Anderson--Malissa Arabel Estes	6
	[wit William Reel]	
May 29 1873	George Cotton--Diana Simpson	66
June 1 1873	Samuel F Crawley--Rosa Luttrell	6
Mar 3 1873	James Allen --Nancy P Crocker	31
May 15 1873	J W Campbell--Mary Otridge	25

Iron County, Missouri Marriages
Book B 1873-1881

| Mar 6, 1873 | Henry Chandler--Betsy Jane Hedric | 2 |

April 4, 1873   Milton Hardridge --Mary Cummel   73

Feb 18, 1873   Jules N Aubuchon--L Emma Thomas   69

June 29 1873   George W Rooker--Mrs Mary Edgar   8

May 11. 1873   Joseph A Jones --Lucinda Douglas   105

May 11 1873   John Clements --Susan A Hall   105

April 10, 1873 Robert Sutton --Mary Martin   101

July 16. 1873   George W Davis-- Lizzie Hancock   6
      [Wit, James Davis & James Townsend   ]
Aug 13. 1873   Lewis Short--Ann Martin   106
      [Wit: Reuben Wyatt & James Townsend   ]
Aug 15 1873   William Mabee--Mrs Missouri E. Philips 122

Feb 9, 1873   John Burton --Nancy M Hawkins   25

Aug 28, 1873   William Davis--Sarah Sutton   33
      [Wit Col J A Dellingham & Christian Heitkamp]
Aug 10, 1873   John F Smith--Sarah Jane Arisman   111

Oct 17, 1872   Charles O Jones--Ella Dee Tong   85
      [groom of Springfield , bride of Ironton]
Sept 4, 1873   John Farrar--Mary Ann Cloud   33

April 8 1873   William W Hughes--Sarah Hartridge   107

Aug 21, 1873   Heinrich Schmidt--Johannette Michel   41

Aug 28 1873   Charley Bettis--Laurina Preslin   106
      [Wit Andy Mathes & Jerry Harden]

June 27 1873   Benjamine F Irvin--Rachel Rice Partese 21

Sept 18, 1873 David B Hawkins--Rachel Campbell   25

Aug 27 1873   John W Neely --Mrs Sarah Warren   25

Oct 2, 1873   Gustav Zude--Mrs Emilia Gankie   41

Aug 10 1873   William Usrey --Sarah Higgens   32

Aug 10, 1873   William Goodman--Nancy Higgens   32

Nov 5 1873   W H Sutton--Narcissey M. Hensen   33

Sept 29 1873 John Sallee--Mary J Burgan   33

Oct 14 1873   Thomas Milton Bell--Mary Theresa Walters 73

Iron County Missouri Marriages
Book B 1873-1881

[groom of Iron Co   bride of St Francois Co.]
Aug 24, 1873   Andrew J Cooper--Lettie Cooper   29

Nov 23, 1873   Rufus Skimmerhon--Mary Hale   33

Aug 7, 1873   Perry C Bay--America Marsters   25

Dec. 25, 1873   John Cronkelton--Monterry Turngate   33
       [Wit Nathan Johnson J T Aker & J L Stevens   ]
Nov 4 1873   M A Doty--Ida Tetwiler   96
       [resident of Mr M Tetwiler in Ironton]
Dec 11 1873   Allen Denwiddy--Ellen Russell   6
       [wit Soloman Lax 7 Moses Lax]
Nov 5 1873   Joseph F Lindsey--Emily Abby Russell   14

Dec 16, 1873   Sidney Low--Susan Bell   73

Nov 5 1873   Samuel B Bellis--Mrs Malinda A Jones   14

Dec. 14, 1873   Robert E Wren--Nancy E Lashley   42

Aug 31 1873   Edward Morez--Clara A Potter   12

Dec. 22, 1873   John W Richey--Susan Norris   105
       [Wit Susan Norris & James M Logan]
Dec 26 1873   Friedrich Fisher--Mary Caroline Kooth   33

Aug 19, 1873   William Marlow--Lucinda Lee   66

Dec 20 1873   John Rogers--Josephine Kennedy   52
  [groom of Iron Mtn   bride of Pilot Knob-Wit C Kasco]
Oct 6 1873   Fritz Lamstedt--Rebecca Martin   101

Jan 4 1874   Augustus J Babcock--Fannie May   48
  [groom of Carerdolet bride of Arcadia   ]
Nov 2 1873   Fountain Campbell Mary Phillips   48
  [At residence of Josepn Philips]
Jan 1 1874   Thomas D Hughes--Marina Jane Mason   111
  [groom of Iron Co , bride of Crawford Co]
Jan 5 1874   John Peterson--Lena Schneieder   33
       [wit Amelia Dinger & Lena Weiss]
Dec 1 1873   Levi Bridgwater--Mary Jane Seaford   99

Jan 6, 1874   George W Lashley--Mrs Harriet Goforth   111

Dec 25 1873   J R Price--W E Breucer   12

Feb 4, 1874   Winfield S Cooper--Mary Jones   46

Feb 16 1874   David Conner--Christina Johnson   46

Feb 26 1874   Henry Pendergraft--Mary A Pendergraft   105
       [Wit James M Logan & Thomas McKinney]
Feb. 22 1874   Theodore Dubs--Sophia Simmons   87

Iron County, Missouri Marriages
Book B 1873-1881

[Wit, L F. Sullivan & Mrs Shaver in Des Arc, Iron Co]
Dec 4 1873   Newton Tims -- Catharine Pinkley   84

Dec 11, 1874   Louis Vandegriss--Ellen Neal   101
   [Wit S A. Shuler]
Jan 18, 1874   John March--Nancy A White   101
   [Wit William White & John Wilson]
Jan 18, 1874   Andrew J. Henson--Lovina J Wauk [Hauk] 105
   { Wit Thomas Reece & Charles Edmonds]
Mar. 5, 1874   John Brickey--Caroline Bird   35

Mar 12, 1874   Adolph Sequist--Fenina Haller   87
   [At residence of Ernst Miller, Annapolis, Wit R A Clark
& A Mannis]
Mar 29 1874   Heinrich Schaaf--Caroline Wallis   86
   [Wit Herman Wallis & F Zeenus
Oct 15, 1873   Henry Schaper--Rika Martin   86
   [Wit Henry Schlueter & R Scheons
Mar 5 1874   Isom Womack --Elizabeth Tomalson   46

Mar 26, 1874   James F Thompson--Matilda Arbee Wiseman 105
   [At W Johnson, wit: Robert Thompson & John Wiseman]
April 9, 1874   Joshua M. Palmerton--Lillie C Layman   36
   [Wit. A C & J. D. Layman & M J. & J C Pinder]

April 9, 1874   John Kline --Mary Dace   6
             [Wit· Mrs Burnell]
April 16 1874 H D Boughen--L E Smith   6
             [Wit. Mrs M Delano]
April 9, 1874   Bernard Krumbholtz--Mena Kocher   86
   [Wit Kasper Kipp & Fred Fisher]
April 16 1874 Charles Martin--Matilda Schmidt   86
   [Wit; Henry Richter & Henry Schlueter]
April 21. 1874   John Wellman-- Fredericka Audelein   86
   [Wit William Beel & William Kessler]
Mar 17, 1873   Jacob S Sisco--Elizabeth McNail   107

Feb 8 1874   Louis Fleischer--Matilda Needner   33
   [Wit, Amelia Dinger & Jacob Grandhomme]
April 26 1874   Philipp Kolb--Mrs. Johanna Pape   41

Mar 8, 1874   William C Westbrook--Flora Huff   66
   [groom of Wayne Co   bride of Iron Co]
April 6 1874   Johann Heinrich Friedrich Rolf--
                            Mrs. Eva Margaretha Rahm 41
April 30 1874   William Miller--Ann Collins   66

May 9 1874   Louis Boerttle--Laura Felica Smith   33
             [Wit Arthur Smith]
Dec 11 1872? John N Thompson --Ellen Hale   78
   [Wit John Thompson & Keziah Thompson 'Note" On next page
in record John H Thompson--Ellen Hale is shown 1874?]

Mar 5, 1874   F M Morris--Mary J Highley   73

[groom of Dent Co. , bride of Iron Co
Mar 12 , 1874   Benjamine F. Kohn--Mary Agnes Vandyke   1
[All of Reynolds Co]
Jan 8 1874   Thomas Christopher--Mary Fears   88

June 15, 1873? Ervin Lane--Sarah L Chitty   88

May 13 1874   Bernard Rutsman-- Mrs Magdalena Schmidt   33

--- 7, 1874   John H Thompson-- Ellen Hale??   86?

June 23 1874   John Meyer--Mrs Dorothea Wickman   41
         [bride formerly Richter]
June 25, 1874   John A Henry--Caroline Riley   105
      [Wit James Riley & Lavinia Riley]
July 12, 1874   Samuel Martin--Josephine Hawkins   65

June 30, 1874   Andrew T Harrison--Julia A Russell   8

June 22, 1874   N M. Ketting --Emma McClary   46

July 9, 1874   Jasper Newton --Isabella Roberson   33

July 19, 1874   Wilhelm Beck--Julia Mund   86
[groom of St Louis , bride of Pilot Knob Wit   Chas Boss
                              & Louis Schwaner]
Nov ? 15, 1874   James Bennett--Mary Stanton   110

April 27, 1874   Samuel C Bellis --Anna Beacon   110

Mar 8, 1874   Nathan Johnson --Maggie Moore   110

July 16 1874   Levi Freeland--Sarah Fuel   110
   [both of Madison Co Mo   ]
July 22, 1874   Daniel H Mac--Sarah F Barnes   110

May 7, 1874   Oliver Twitty--Mary Welch   105
   [both of Madison Co Mo]
July 20, 1874   Charles Asher--Diena Byrs   3

Aug 10, 1874   James F Jordon-- Cerina Lagrana   33

Aug 11, 1874   William Montgomery--Martha Stanalania   46
   [married at Pull Tight, Iron Co]
Aug 8, 1874   William Hill- Emma Newman   110
   [Wit Thomas Newman & John Newman]
June 18, 1874   J M Johnson --[name not given]   6
   [Wit M C Ayers   Index --M J Albert]
Aug 17, 1874   Joseph Eger--Emma Kaiser   86
   [groom of Granite Quary Iron Co. bride of St Louis]
   [Wit., Val Effinger & Charles Base]
Aug 16 1874   Houston A Turner--Callie Shepherd   33

Sept 3, 1874   William Philipps--Wilhelmina Hofmeister   86

Iron County, Missouri Marriages
Book B 1873-1881

[Wit Henry Behrens & Mina Ahrens]
Sept 16 1874   Andrew M Figart-- Rachel Powel   33

Oct 2, 1874   James Ellis --Hannah Armstrong   35

July 19. 1874   Edward Brown--Harriet Williams   77

Aug 8, 1874   James K Wallis --Mathilda Davidson   70

Sept 30 1874   J D Simmonds--Anna J Simmonds   66

Oct 29, 1874   William Hay-- Lucy Peas   87
     [Wit William J Russell & Miss Rebecca Russell]
Nov 11, 1874   Andrew H Fisher --Della M. Harris   14

Oct. 22, 1874   John Long --Harriet Pratt   88

Nov 24 1874   Richard Viesterson--Mary Marcella Burks   87
     [Wit Thomas Martin & Franklin Woods]
Nov 5 1874   Willis Chamber-- Darcus A Hedric   2

Nov 5 1874   John Bears--Mary Willhite   2

Dec 7, 1874   Blanton Bollinger--Emily Shafer   34

Nov 3 1874   John Puhljon--Mary Nelson   33

Dec 3, 1874   Andrew Jackson Mays-Amanda Adoline Geisler33

Oct 15 1874   George DeWitt--Mrs Sarah L Forster   33

Dec 15, 1874   William M Key --Kinzziah Dunn   74

Dec 18 1874   Robert McKenzie-- Sarah A Weise   33

Sept 3, 1874   George W Smith -- Philena Miller   100

Oct 11 1874   James M Crocker--Martha Ann Maret   31

Sept 27, 1874   J R Beers--M F Wood   43

Dec 17. 1874   Isaam Fuller-- Nancy Ellis   66

Jan 3. 1875   Reuben Thomas --Mrs Harriet Wiatt   105
     [Wit Daniel Leech & Susan Leach]
Jan 25, 1875   William Hart--Bettie Sutton   33

Dec 11 1874   Nelson G Clayton--Drucilla L C Akers   118

Jan 24, 1875   Ellis R Moore--Arte M Adams   111

Dec 24, 1874   Jesse Hawkins--Mary Wilson   63

Feb 9. 1875   Edward Paris Edwards-Almarintha C Hasting33

Iron County, Missouri Marriages
Book B 1873-1881

Feb   2, 1875   Lawerance Cotter--Susan Cox   33

Oct   11 1874   James M Crocker -- Martha Ann Maret   31

Sept 3, 1874   William Phillips--Wilhedmana Huffmuster   86
    [Wit   Henry Behrens & Marie Ahrens]
Aug   8, 1874   James K Wallas--Susan Matilda Davison   70

Sept 3 1874   George W. Smith--Philena Miller   101

Feb   2 1875   Lawrence Cotter --Susan Cox   33

Feb   14 1875   Columbus Hilderbrand--Laura Reynolds   14

Feb. 16, 1875   Hilliary A Fletcher--Sadie F Ringo   14

Feb   25 1875   Joseph Henry Sutton--Susan Martin   101

Dec   31, 1874   Milford C Warren -- Pamelia J Wiseman   73

Jan   25. 1875   Felan B Stephens--Josephine Fendygriff   3

Mar   4. 1875   John H Angle--Malinda J. Snead   3
    [At house of Columbus Tindle]
Mar   9 1875   J Henderson --Matilda J Snead   25

Mar   28 1875   Daniel Lewis-- Christa Ann Stephenson   95

Jan   22 1875   Francis Conor--Permilia Jane Allison   67
   [A residence of Mr. Cape Ballard]

Mar   12, 1875   James Henderson--Margarett D Winengar   105
   [Wit Kelly Thomas & George Wineger]
Mar   13, 1875   George Baxter--Margaret Harbison   71

Jan   18 1875   Alfred Proffitt--Lizzie Davis   40

April 17 1875   Aaron Lear--Cordelia Isabella Barton   14

Mar   11 1875   Lewis George--Mrs Rachel Hawkins   14

April 1 1875   Isaac Brewer --Eveline Hale   66

May 9 1875   Charles L Heckman--Emily H Clifton   114

May 9 1875   Charles Williams--Mary Robbs   58
   [residence of Lewis Buckner]
May 16 1875   James G Austin --Sallie C Medley   33
   [Wit James Beard & Wm A Fletcher]
Feb 27 1875   Jeramiah Denison--Elivabeth A Harbison   118

June 13 1875   Stephen Tulleck--Lucinda Baker   24

Iron County, Missouri Marriages
Book B 1873-1881

May 24 1875	Rondey S. Legget -- Annie Howe	110
[Wit Dr Minor & W McFarland]		
June 24, 1875	Benjamine C Taber--Annie Mayfield	33
June 15, 1875	Carril Ratlif--Lucinda Mead	62
April 18, 1875	James Campbell--Sarah Reed	101
Aug 14, 1875	Abraham Abernathy--Charlotte Bollinger	33
Aug 19, 1875	James Murry--Mary Gilmn	34
Aug 26, 1875	Simon E Buford --Eliza A. Packard	110
[Wit . W & T Beucheman]		
July 1 1875	Louis Arnold - Maria Dreyer	41
Sept 20, 1875	Harvy Johnson--Mary L Ganter	33
Sept 20, 1875	Daniel Scrutchfield--Elvira Bone	33
Sept 29, 1875	George McClany--Eliza J Young	--
Sept 29, 1875	George D Baxter--Margaret Stout	--
June 29, 1875	James R Spencer--Mary E Tindell	118
Nov 5, 1875	James H Kelly --Sarah C Anderson	34
Sept. 23, 1875	Joseph Duncan--Elizabeth Norris	19
Nov 10, 1875	Benjamine Nance--Martha Jane Kaiser	33
July 18 1875	Partick Hanlen--Catherine Fanney Casey	51
[Wit Patrick Doyle & Mrs Burke]		
Dec 19 1875	Franklin J Stevenson --Mary Lewis	95
July 21, 1875	Robert Mayhugh--Mrs Mary Bradshaw	109
Dec 29 1875	Isiah Collins-- Lucinda Jane Johnson	61
Dec 28 1975	August Gehse--Augusta Kanoholz	41
Jan 23 1876	J M Kelly--Drucilla C Rhoades	34
Jan 5 1876	Goel Clark--Miss O F Loyd	9
Jan 6. 1876	President White-- Matilda Mathis	20
Feb 12, 1876	P C Goodman--Emily E Sternel	114
Jan 6 1876	James B Edward--Jolina Jaycox	40
Jan 7 1876	William B Newman--Sarah Luella Hughes	40

Iron County Missouri Marriages
Book B 1873-1881

Mar   2 1876   Henry Earls-- Lizzie Deubo   78

Feb   27. 1876   George Morrison --Jeminaih Wilbank   58
        [groom of Madison Co ,Bride of Iron Co]
Mar   8. 1876   Paul Patton --Aurabell Kesling   40

Mar   9. 1976   John T Crew--Sarah Elizabeth Hendrich   40
        [groom of Franklin Co , bride of Iron Co]
April 2, 1876   Henry Inman --Martha Nicholson   95

Mar   22 1876   John A Horton --Martha J Woods   4

Feb   22, 1876   Thomas Jackson --Eliza Jane Studham   95

Feb   28 1876   John B Belmar--Mrs Conaly Smith   77

April 9, 1876   Izikiah Branda--Catherine Lewis   82

June 20, 1876   Riley Falkner--Susan Canada   31

June 20, 1876   Soloman Nellson--Amanda Crocker   31

May 5, 1876   Daniel Kerterson--Rebecca Justice   66

July 24, 1876   A G Smith--Jane Murphy   33

June 24, 1876   Mosly Vest--Elizabeth Allen   5

April 27 1876   William H Baker--Eda C Adams   5

July 17 1876   James Reed --Mrs Ardelia Boyd   114

July 15, 1876   Peter Goodman--Sarah Game?   95

Nov   20 1876   John A Monroe--Sarah Cox   33

April 11, 1876   George Goodman--Mrs Mary Edwards   95

June 28 1876   Leland Lester Myers--Mrs Olive Sizemore 73

Sept 8 1876   Steven D Sutton--Mandy Davis   33

July 9. 1876   George Sullivan--Adda Sherrill   82

Sept. 17, 1876   Riley Steadham--Margaret Ann Messer   61
        [at residence of the late Joseph Hampton. Esc Wit
         John B Hampton & Thomas J Hampton]
Feb   26 1876   Peter Prow--Elizabeth C Beavers   93

July 10. 1876   Calvins Simmons--Ann Crossland   101

Nov   26 1876   John A Monroe--Sarah Cox   33

Nov   26 1876   Robert Huff-- Elizabeth McNeely   58

Iron County, Missouri Marriages
Book B 1873-1881

Oct 1 1876   N A Farr--Melissa Chilton   95
   [both of Wayne Co Mo]
Oct 19, 1876   Peter Algeyer--Annie Lotz   58

Oct. 19, 1876   George Sherrill--Mary J Pinkley   58

Oct 29, 1876   Franklin Charleton-- Mary Reed   95

Dec. 10, 1876   Moses Hawkins--Mrs Jane Lee   104

Nov 15, 1876   Thomas C Brown--Lizzie Ake   50
   [groom from Carter Co   bride from St Francois Co.]
Sept 23, 1876   Willis Hall--Polly M Crocker   31

Dec. 21, 1876   James M Duncan--Margaret Wood   66

Feb 4, 1876?   John W Miller--Darkey Angelina King   19

Dec 25, 1876   John C Clark--Mary W Hofner   91

Jan 11, 1877   Robert M. Thompson--Julie Thompson   91

Feb 14, 1877   Charles B Valle Jr.--Alice Edison   105
   [groom of Madison Co ,bride of Wash Co Wit   Charles B
Valle Sr & Nancy Valle]
Feb. 22, 1877   James D Gleason--Mary L. Smith   34

Feb 28 1877   Lilimon Lewis Collins--Carrie A Preston 34
   [" both are descendants of Ham " [colored]
Feb 27, 1877   Alfred Buckner--Minnie Van Hess   48
   [both of Madison Co , At A Martins in Iron Co]
April 2, 1877   Claudius N Powell--Frances Conway   64

Jan. 14, 1877   George W Brewer--Tempa P Chapman   11
   [at residence of Green Brewer Wit   William Terrill &
William Kirkpatrick]
Jan 17 1877   Reuben Thomas Jr --Agnes A Whitsett   11

Dec 23, 1877?   Francis J Henderson--Mary Logan   93
   [attn should read 1876 --filed April 1877]
Dec 21 1875?   John W Harrol--Fannie George   93

April 11 1876?   J A. Logan --Ternora Neely   93

Mar 22 1876?   Miles Redding --Louisa L Graham   66

April 2 1877   August Hermann Jauke--
                         Catherine Wilhelmina Schmidt   83
May 29 1877   James Cuthbert--Semanthe C Fitzpatrick   64
   [Wit A Bealey]
Mar 8 1877   Louis H Johnson--Mellissa Miller   58

April 26 1877   John W Allcorn--Sarah C Sutton   114

63

April 1, 1877   Isaac Smith-- Jane Finton   58

April 1 1877   James Rouse --Elizabeth Stephenson   58

April 22, 1877   James M King-- Mary J Stevenson   94
     [groom of Madison Co , bride of Iron Co.]
April 22 1877   James L Collins --Mary J King   94

Mar   29, 1877   Jackson Razor--Talitha L McTadden   58

July 4, 1877   Harvey Boon---Julia Hayden   110
     [groom of San Francisco Ca , bride of Iron Co. Wit
     W A Lyman & L C Bellis]
July 1 1877   Wallis Keatherly--Sarah Ann Wallis   62

Mar   1, 1877   George Justice--- Mary J Mead   62

May 26 1877   James h Sutterfield --Martha A Reeves 11
     [Wit   James Hughes & Thomas Stout]

Dec   24, 1874?   William McCall--Jennie Edmonds   33

Oct   28, 1876   Andy Cooley -- Harriet Tullock   33

Nov   28 1876   Amos J Walp--Mrs Phoebe McQuire   33

Dec   4 1876?   James R Canning --Mrs Mary E Bennett 33

Dec   15 1876   Mitchell Center --D Caroline Cagel   33

Feb   6. 1877   Philip Pariso-- Emma Breitenstein   33

Mar   27 1877   Willis Singleton--Arintha Bradshaw   33

April 2, 1877   S M Meeks---Miss E A Curtis   33

July 26 1877   John Behm--Louise Schlucter   33

Aug   8. 1877   David Taul--Jane Cummingham   33

May 30 1863?   Lewis Bales--Sarah Agien   72
     [by Chaplain of 3rd Mo Cav U S Vol]
Mar   22 1876   Miles Pedding --Louise L Graham   66

Oct   25, 1877   James W Russell--Mrs Telitha J Meddus 95

Oct   21 1877   George C Bowls--Mary J Gibson   95

Dec   23, 1877   Mathew w Baily--Rachael Hawkins   11

July 26 1877   William Gilmore--Luvina Huff   58
     [at residence of William Huff Sr]
July 4, 1877   James Faulkner --Sarah Ann Warren   31

Iron County, Missouri Marriages
Book B 1873-1881

Aug   5 1877   Henry Ruble --Kizzie Lewis   95

Sept. 19, 1877   Monroe House--Racheal Dennis   105

Sept 19 1877   William J Smith--Geneva C Curtis   50
                    [house of brides father, Smith Curtis]
Sept 9, 1877   Andrew Ruble--Kizzie Lewis   114

Oct 16, 1877   Andrew J. Harviell--Florence Lee   64
                    [Wit · William Fletcher & Lucy Evans]
Aug 2, 1877   William H Greenwood--Mary A. Reed   118

Aug 5 1877   William Treadaway--Mollie Bellor   58

Nov 1, 1877   William Willson--Sarah Jane Belmar   76

Nov 15, 1877   S Samuel Goins-- Sarah Jane McHenniss   55

Aug 2, 1877   Joseph Hendrick--Sarah Parker   31

Mar. 9, 1876?   J C Hornsey-- Mary A Williams   44

Dec 26, 1877   Jr Grims--Veleta J Marlin   114

Nov 4 1877   James C Cox--Catherine Norton   105
                    [Wit , John D Greason & Hewitt Greason]
Sept 20 1877   Andrew Vandegrif--Missouri Smith   101

Jan. 1, 1878   Leonard L Peck--Annie M Gray   34

Dec 18 1877   Albert Buxton --Elvira A Lomas   79

Oct 30, 1877   John M Hook--Emily F Rutledge   81
                    [at residence of William Rutledge]
Jan 23, 1878   Poul Dupri--Lillian Lingham   52

Jan 27 1878   James Sollar--Catherine Wilhite   2
                    [Wit . J L Midget & T J Wilhite]
Feb 14, 1878   John Mehagan--Mrs Mary Newbery   34

Feb 14 1878   Leo Roth--Rosa Sing   33

Nov 16 1877   Thomas Yarbaugh-- Anna West   58

Nov 16 1877   M C Markwell--Celia Allen   58

Feb 11 1878   James Watson McFaddlin--Polly Sutton   95

Feb 17 1878   William Marchbanks--Sarah Jane Coble   95
                    [groom of Wayne Co   bride of Iron Co   ]
Feb 10 1978   J Y Crocker--Glorina D Merrit   37

Feb 10 1878   Richard C Crocker--Sofrana L. Martin   37

Nov 15 1877   John Y Mayfeel--Margaret Reed   31

Feb 14 1878   Franklin G Reeves--Emma M Stephenson   50
    [at Reeves Stephenson father of bride]
Jan   6, 1878   David Stephenson--Martha Russell   19

Jan 13, 1878   Monterey P Belcher--Mary E Ferguson   84

Jan 27 1878   Wiley Oneal--Lester G. Boles   94

Feb 20 1878   Thomas M Williams --Catherine Evans   33

Dec 16, 1877   William Kelly--Jane Wadlow   27
          [at house of Nancy Wadle]
Feb 26, 1878   Daniel VanCurren--Jane Hinson   66

Jan 20 1878   Jasper Dunn--Florence Knight   66

Dec 15, 1877   Henry Wilson--Rody Buckner   58

Dec 18. 1877   George Swanegan--Catherine Sherrell   58

Feb 16, 1878   Jerry Hickman --Eliza Eldrige   32

Mar 10 1878   Marion Irvin --Mary Hill   79

April 21, 1878   Gilbert Johnson--Catherine Hale   66

Mar 17 1878   Frank Woods--Louisanna Casey   19

Mar 30 1878   James A Chapman--Alberta A Thompson   37

May 19 1878   Andrew Huff--Mollie Graham   66

May 7, 1878   Tennissee C Lovens--Mary M Clubb   34

May 2 1878   William Dunn--Charloty Key   55

Mar 14, 1878   Issac W Nichols--Annie McCue   95
     [groom of Madison Co   bride of Iron Co]
Mar 21 1878   William A Huff--Stacy Ann Ruble   95

July 14 1878   William T Levey-- Nancy Arnold   23
     [groom or Wayne Co   bride of Iron Co]
July 30 1878   Silas E Panebecker--Mary D Campbell   92

Mar 3 1878   F M Lemen--Amanda P Bowles   96

Aug 9 1878   William J Cole--Catherine Omohondro   96
     [at residence of R Omohondro Iron Co]
Aug 4 1878   James London--Mary E Reed   --
     [groom of Iron Co   bride of Wayne Co]
Sept 26 1878   Columbus C Brewington--Mary Arnett   19

Oct 17, 1878	William Warren--Mamie Maybury	60
Sept 3, 1878	Walter Fisher--Emma Dequire	48
Sept 19, 1878	Millard F Lowe--Mary Elmira Spencer	--
July 11, 1878	Henry Pinkley--Jane Buckner	58
	[groom of Reynolds Co , bride of Iron Co]	
Oct 13, 1878	John Westly Arms-Lydia Armstrong [colored]	34
Nov 1 1878	Robert Williams--Martha Evans	104
Oct 3, 1876	John Brewer--Eva Brewer	66
	[groom of Reynolds Co bride of Iron Co]	
Oct 24, 1878	Levi Knees--Lucinda E Cowan	105
Nov 7 1878	E P Keach--Julia M Russell	26
	[groom of Bollinger Co , bride of Iron Co]	
Nov 4 1878	James M Fitzpatrick--Frances Edmonds	105
Nov 1, 1878	James C Russell--Mattie Hill	81
Jan 16, 1878	Rober F Thompson--Mary C Acres	30
Dec 22, 1878	John M Swiney--- Mary Eliza Thompson	30
	[groom of Dent Co bride of Iron Co]	
Feb 8, 1879	Charles Schluter--Fredericka Wolf	33
Jan 19 1879	B W Revelle---Mrs Joanna E Morrison	33
Feb 13, 1879	Henry C Bell--Julia F Wyatt	14
Feb 22 1879	Mathew Gowan--Fannie Hampton	32
Feb 25, 1879	Massey Ruble--Susan E Fokis	32
Feb 12, 1879	George Sutherlin--Elvira Kelly	104
	[groom of Farmington ,bride of Iron Co]	
Jan 22 1879	George C Loomis-- Emily A Love	107
	[Wit Samuel Lucas & Dalliason Love]	
Dec 5 1878	George Henson--Maggie Lotz	57
Dec 26, 1879	William Nance--Susan Kitcherside	57
Jan 23 1879	George Southerland--Nancy Buckner	57
April 3 1879?	Stacey Bell--Mary A Harbison	34
Jan 13 1879	Dee? Snodgrass--Mrs Lucy Proffit	55
April 17 1879	Henry Sutton--Laura Martin	16
May 7 1879	Michael Muller--Judy Caroline Sizemore	79

Date	Names	Page
May 11 1879	Ulysus A Miller--Lucy M Seal	92
Feb 24 1879	Henry R Henderson--Eda C Adams	37
Feb 5. 1879	John F Steevens--Malinda J Logan	81
May 11. 1879	Franklin Clay Semands-Safrona Jane Clifton	65
Feb 18. 1879	John H Hamilton--Sariot Campbell	94
April 6. 1879	William O'Neal--Manearvy Raney	94
Mar 30. 1879	Charles A Matkin--Anney E Kelley	94
June 4 1879	Joseph Shaver--Mary Russell	102

[At the colored M E. Church at Ironton]

Date	Names	Page
June 15. 1879	Robert B McCalister--Mary J Holland	34
June 18. 1879	John Harty--Salley Bone	45
July 4 1879	James F Chandion--Alice J Razor	16
April 9, 1879	John C Yates--Nancy Williams	107

[Wit Albert McMurty & John C Williams]

Date	Names	Page
July 10, 1879	Bernard Johle--Mary Turner	34
May 11 1879	George Ketcherside--Martha Jane Lewis	58
May 8 1879	Adolf Loez--Belle Casteel	58
May 11 1879	Samuel Beeman--Cinderella J Lewis	37
Aug 10 1879	James M Lloyd--Elizy Ann Stevenson	27
Aug 24. 1879	Marellus T D Campbell--Lula J Raser	92

[residence of Jacob Raser's, Iron Co]

Date	Names	Page
July 9 1879	Walter W Nall--Florence Sanner	14
Sept 23. 1879	August Aubersmith--Martha Brown	45
Oct 2 1879	Hermann Zude--Emma Friederika Elizabeth Will	22
Aug 17, 1879	William Barnes--Ellen Harbison	71
Oct 4 1879	Joel Kelly--Nancy Ellen Randolph	13
Oct 2, 1879	Jacob Nines--Emeline Thomason	33
Sept 10 1879	Moses Lax--Isabella Krumph	102
Oct 2 1879	Peter Ruhl--Jane Buford	11
Sept 12 1879	William Terrill--Mrs Mary Farley	11

Aug 3 1879	Jacob Pettyjohn--Elizabeth Buckner	66
Sept 28, 1879	William E Westerman--Sarah A Adams	37
Oct 26, 1879	William T Gilliam--Zina J. Bryan	37
Oct. 15, 1879	Solomon Harris--Elizabeth Sutton	33
Nov 14 1879	John Brooks--Armintha Lee	33
Nov 4, 1879	Ferdinand Stemme--America Copeland	33
Aug 25, 1879	John Purkiner--Phebe Louis	55
Nov 23, 1879	King Moses--Jane Trollinger	118
Nov 25, 1879	Samuel Weast--Mrs Lizzie Creel	17
Dec 3, 1879	George A. Smith--Lizzie Gilliam	68
Dec 3 1879	Reuben Lee Moore--Bertha Moyer	103
Nov. 6, 1879	B W Wesley--N. D Goddis	34
Nov 17 1879	William B Smith-- Martha O StClair	92
Mar 14, 1880?	Joseph M Stagner--Virginia Kemper	19
[filed April 13 1880]		
Oct. 27, 1879	William Henson--Mary Pratt	47
[Wit A J Dewitt & Mary Dewitt		
Oct 1, 1879	John Wiett--Victory Leage	47
[Wit Reuben Thomas Sr & Reuben Thomas Jr]		
Nov 16, 1879	James E Moss--Leanney M Rubel	114
Dec 11 1879	Franklin Maybel--Lilly Baird	53
[Wit Giles Russell & J W Berryman]		
Dec 8 1879	E T Jennings--Eliza Brent	111
Dec 24, 1879	Jacob Tomlinson--Mary Shrum	91
Nov 20 1879	Philip Mayfield--Cora Adaline Reed	31
Jan 8 1880	Nelson Bell--Mary E Harbison	71
Jan 27 1880	William Cooper--Annie Turner	68
Feb. 1 1880	Edward W Miller--Desinia Seals	19
Jan 12 1880	William Lester--Rebecca J Morris	19
Feb 10, 1880	Henry Rapp--Tnilda Reel	33
Feb 11 1880	John Welch--Mrs Kate Griffith	33

Feb 2, 1880   Adolph Kirchner--
                  --Mrs Catharina Hortman, Nee Hills   33
Feb 16, 1880   Thomas Jones --Ellen Jamison   33

Jan 25 1880   George Anderson--Mary A Doll   122

Feb 26, 1880   John S McDowell--Belle Hill   47
   [Wit. Lizzie Graham & Mattie Hancock]
Dec 29 1879   Joseph Bradley--Rebecca Moore   118

Jan 25, 1880   James Sutton--Mary Blantonship?   66

Mar 4, 1880   John Ruhl--Abijah Sutton   33

Feb 24, 1880   James H Elgin--Sarah Jane Evans   49
   [groom of Farmington, bride of Belleview, Iron Co
Mar 16, 1880   Thomas H Moore-- Jennie Harvey   54
   [Wit Messrs Edgar, Shepard, Harvey and others]
Mar 21, 1880   Louis Vandergrift--Mrs Cynthia Lamburt 54
   [Wit Hon J W Berryman, W H Rose and others]

April 3, 1880   Allen Tullock--Diana Cotton [colored]   34

Jan 25, 1880   Boyd T Orr--Martha Seal   58

April 11, 1880   Stephen Smith--Jane Buckner   66

April 11, 1880   Elijah D Holloway-Mrs Harriet McCollough65

April 14 1880   Thompson Dunnegan--Sally C Foguaide   65

April 12, 1880   Jacob Batzle--Louisa Oesh   71

May 23, 1880   Daniel R Good--Lizzie Bell Holon   16

Mar 29, 1880   Martin V Holt--Martha A Hedsketh   11

Dec 20, 1879   George W Walles-- Martha A Bearsher   94

July 20 1879   Samuel Lewis--Elizabeth Bradey   94
   [groom of Iron Co   bride of Madison Co]
Oct 19 1879   Joseph A Lashley--Lilly H Carey   94

April 18 1880   John Spragley--Elizabeth Horton   94

Mar 8 1880   Joseph Andrew Thompson-Mary Liviney Sumpter
                                                           15
June 6 1880   Simon Carter--Artis Johnson [colored] 34

April 11 1880   Thomas Tesrow--Jane C Smith   7

June 6 1880   Charles Clifton --Vira Huff   32
       [only dates given is the filing date]

Iron County, Missouri Marriages
Book B 1873-1881

June 16 1880   D. B Hockman --Elizabeth Huff   32
     [only date given is filing date]
June 16, 1880   W J Wolf-- Nancy Simmons   32
        [only date is filing date]
June 17, 1880   Daniel Hastings--Mary Corbien   119
    [Wit Mary Corbien, Chas Corbien and Elsie Reed]
July 15, 1880   Sam Belmar--Kate Allgier   16

July 28, 1880   Jeff Cooper--Addie Allen   33

July 4 1880   William Monroe Cummings--Catherine Stone 33

July 5, 1880   Thomas Hendricks--Mrs Ellen Myers   33

July 18. 1880   Joseph E Fulcher--Louisa Lowry   33

July 3 1880   Frank Fitzgibbens--Annie Cogan   33

May 6, 1880   Henry Schlieter--Amilan Amanda Mitchel   33

May 22 1880   L J Luthon--Malinda Knapp   33

May 21 1880   John Mayes-- Francis Wamack   33

April 9. 1880   Douglass Walters --Mary Johnson   33

May 17. 1880   Henry Bodine --Anna Merritt   33

April 29, 1880   Adolph Aubuchon--Josephine Clark   33

Mar 30. 1880   Thomas J Clark--Eliza F Thomas   33

Mar 15. 1880   Joseph A Gregory--Adele Gratiot   33

Aug 28 1880   George Adell--Emma Rust   33

July 9, 1880   James T Kimes --Nancy A T. Davis   19

April 16 1880   Sirus Lawson--Nancy Dunn   55

June 27 1880   Walker Bone--Ettie Heaston   55

July 25 1880   Francis Torcus Rudy--Ida Schultz   119
    [Wit George Schultz & Louise Schmids]
Aug 8 1880   John Dunn --Margaret Breslin   119

May 16 1880   Thedor Lotz--Fannie Baker   58

Aug 8 1880   Jeff Razor--Emma Bumgardner   16

Aug 22 1880   James E Pinkley--Frankie J Robb   92
     [at residence of William E Robb]
Sept 2. 1880   Jules L Rudy-- Elsie E Cooper   98

71

[at residence of Mrs M J Harviell Arcadia]
Aug   2   1880   Robert G   Pormer--Mary Jane Belcher   33

Sept 8. 1880   S   D   Myer--Rosselle Schneider   33

Aug   26 1880   Richard Burk--Elizabeth Roan   33

Sept 16, 1880   Jacob M Mayer--Lucy Campbell   33

Sept 16 1880   Edon Gaston-- Alice Shrum   33

Sept 19, 1880   Thomas Connell--Mrs Mary Hammer   33

Aug   1 1880   Flavius Clark Hyde--Mary Lucinda Coble   65

Aug   15, 1880   David W Raney--Lou Bursheer   65

Sept 19 1880   James Cromstalk--Elizabeth Shelton   94

Sept 16, 1880   Carl Erbe--Augusta Pauline Louise Guse   18
   [groom of Wachtersbach. Kurhessen, Germany·
                   bride of DramsburgPommern. Prussen Germany]
Oct   7 1880   August Alleve--Wilhemine Louise Peetz   18
   [groom of Bokeneur, Hanover Germany, bride of Cape G. Co
     Wit   Anne Peetz Percv Schubert,,Helene Gockel, Henry
Walon & Adelheid Grandhomme]
Sept -- 1880   William J Gooman--Nancy E Allison   94

Aug   29 1880   James Shreave--Josephine Casteel   4

Oct   2 1880   James Clark --Nancy E Smith   116

Oct   14 1880   J   T Carter--Alice Mayberry   17

Aug   15 1880   Henry H Brewington--Sarah Russell   123

Sept 16 1880   J T T Lufry--Miss m G Deboard   59
    [at residence of Y V O'Bannon]
Oct   5, 1880   William P Edgar--Pressia S Whitworth   38

July 4 1880   John Lucy--Lucinda Hubble   66

Oct   17 1880   Anthony Foster-- Laurena Williams   66

Nov   23 1860   George Miles Palmer--Amelia Schmidz   119
    [Wit   George Schultz &Louisa Schmidt   ]
Nov   23 1880   George Schultz--Louisa Schmidt   119
    [Wit   George Miles Palmer & Amelia Palmer]

Aug   1 1880   John S Collins-- Mary Omohondro   97

Sept 29 1880   Calvin Chapman--Eliza M Bryan   37

Nov   21 1880   Freeman Hayward--Darkus Campbell   122

Iron County, Missouri Marriages
Book B 1873-1881

Oct 1 1880   Charles E Davis --Chareta Ann Johnson   55

Oct 12, 1880   J A Rivers--Sarah Elizabeth Counts   55

Aug 24, 1880   Benjamine Goverow--Laura Heaston   55

Sept. 1, 1880   Louis N Wallis-- Sarah A Carter   47
   [Wit   A C Hancock, Martha Hancock & G. W Thompson]
Nov 28, 1880   John Loyd--Mary Owen   28
   [At the residence of Thomas Loyd]
Nov 18, 1880   Josiah D Mann--Vill? M Johnson   28

Oct 14 1880   James M Davis --Ellen J Henson   28

Dec 5, 1880   John Jameson--Nancy Russell   65

Nov 7 1880   William J Bollinger --Amelia J Finley   56

Dec. 9, 1880   William Alson Stricklin--Emily Hawk   3
   [at residence of Nelson Hawk]
Dec 12, 1880   Robison Lewis--Marcha J Nance   56

Sept 16, 1880   Amon Palymale--Patsey Black   56

Oct 14, 1880   Jeff Mundy--Sarah A Bebee   10

Dec 30 1880   Benjamine B Myer-Mrs Margaret A Inman 39
   [groom of Iron Co , bride of Madison Co]
Dec. 21 1880   Louis Graham--Sarah Philepha   17

Sept 23, 1880   James M Hickman--Mrs Mary A Sutton   11

Dec 2, 1880   Levi M. Flowers---Mrs -----Miller   11

Dec 30, 1880   Eugene M Logan --Fannie L Reyburn   81

Oct 21 1880   Henry Nelson--Manda E Crocker   121

Oct 14 1880   Oskar S Colt--Mahala Payne   31
   [at house of Edward Payne]
Sept 30, 1880   Hasting Matkirs--Susse? E Carter   58
   [groom of St Francois Co   bride of Iron Co.]
Sept 20 1880   James Scallon-- Nancy W [No Name]   34

July 15 1879   William Tranernicht--
                             Friedericka Henriette Block 33
May 15, 1880   Balentine B Bunnell--May Musson   54
[parties belong to a traveling group exhibiting in Ironton
wit   L B. Miller St. Louis, Lizzie Selkink, Arcadia]

Oct 2 1880   Newton Code--Matilda McGuire   34

Oct 14, 1880   Willis Fisher --Eva Lotz   33

Iron County, Missouri Marriages
Book B 1873-1881

Nov 18, 1880   Daniel Brooks-- Mollie Fritzwater   33

Sept 23 1880   A P Vance--Agnes Murphy   33

Nov 25, 1880   Coleman Hill--Julia Schmitz   33

Oct 10 1880   John Robert Deve--Looving Church   33

Oct 15, 1880   Henry James--Julia Ann Smith   33

Oct 17 1880   Ranson Breman --Mrs Lucinda Arnwav   33

Oct 23, 1880   Lewis Burns?--Josie Creath   33

Dec 14. 1880   Henry Pemond--Sarah Josephine O'Leary   119
[groom son of Emil Pemond & Augustinar Worille, bride dau of
dennis O'Leary & Delphimar O'Learey, both parties from French
Village , St Francois Co]

Nov 2, 1880   Henry L. Simms--Martha G. Hugh   75
    [groom of St Francois Co ,Bride of Iron Co]
Dec 22. 1880   J A Vineyard-- Miss N M Clark   4

Nov 4, 1880   James Wiley--Mary E. Shrum   47

Dec 30 1880   James Goggin --Sarah Elizabeth Bell   120
     [at residence of Letty Goggin]
Jan 9 1881   William Hyde--Catherine Joyce   119
    [groom of Boston , son of William Hyde and Helen Lynch,
bride of Des Arc, Dau of John Joyce & Mary Sullivan-Wit
Edward & Margaret Logan]

Dec 11 1880   John Williams-- Mary Workhauser   33

Dec 9, 1880   Louis Schwaner--Anna Dewke?   33

Dec 9 1880   James Wallace--Jane Vaughn   27
    [house of William Foster , Iron Co]
Feb 24 1881   Franklin Mcan--Mary Ann Campbell   122

Dec 25 1872?   Joseph Sam Bollinger--Margaret Sutton   57

Feb 14 1877?   J W Coleman--Samanthy Bollinger   67

Dec 25 1880   George Reeves--Emily Campbell   57

Dec 17 1876?   Newton Huff--Leuvany Pinkley   67

Feb 15 1881   William Miller--Martha Kaufman   57

Nov 1 1873?   Thomas Campbell--Mary Reeves   67

Feb 27 1881   Henry Steward--Mat Rouse   66

Iron County, Missouri Marriages
Book B 1873-1881

Feb 10, 1881   Robert C Love --Elizabeth Ella Bryan   3
    [At house of Dolison Love]
Feb 10, 1881   John R McKinney Jr --
                          Pernelia Adaline Hodges 81
Mar 15, 1881   Luther Hill--Lucy E Evans   117

Mar 27, 1881   James Keel--Martha A Maise   47
    [Wit   William Maise, Martha Mase/ & Alex Graham]

Mar 20, 1881   Christian Schaefer--Mary Ida Thomi   119
[groom the son of Chas Schaefer & Claudentia Reimling, born
in Laugencrucken Bruchsal Baden , bride the dau of John
Thomi & Vronica Baier, born in Upstads, Brachsal Baden--Wit
Louis Schaefer & Theresa Inman]

April 6, 1881   A Hall--Ellen Sweeney   33

Jan 30, 1881   John Brooks--Jane Mayes   33

Jan 30, 1881   Francis Sharp--Nancy Oliver   33

Feb 10, 1881   Charles Arnoldi--Nanna Shultz   33

April 6, 1881   L D Jamison-- Mrs Mary Garrett   33

Jan 13, 1881   Samuel P Reyburn--Sallie A Wiatt   81

Jan 24, 1881   D S Love-- Sarah J Bryan   10

Mar 10 1881   F M Lewis --Marthey M Jackson   94

Dec 23, 1881   Theodore Bohms--Elise Hillomen   118
    [groom of st. Francois Co   bride of Iron Co]
April 24, 1881   Charles Roberson --Mrs Alsey Norris   115
    [Wit. James Casteel & August Kellerman]

May 22, 1881   Augustus Clinton Babcock--Pauline Bebee 124

May 12 1881   James M Campbell--Sarah J Sutton   92

June 3, 1881   J W King-- Nancy J Crocker   34

May 24, 1881   Jonathan Clinton--Cordelia Delashmit   113

May 22, 1881   Beryaman Rauft--Bertha Kamhoby   18
    [Wit   Friedrick Ficht August Guse & Anna Rauft]

June 19, 1881   James Tredway--Kizzale J Bounds   65

June 23 1881   Harry P Delaney--Mary Fountaine   33

May 29, 1881   Richard Oaks--Jane Henson   33

April 21 1881   William Welmer-- Henriette Burgsmueller   33

May 7 1881	Edward Langegger--Mrs Margaretha Joos	33
June 6, 1881	L J Keenan--Lena Breitenstein	33
May 22 1881	James Cook--Sarah Marshall	33
April 20, 1881	John Anthony--Lovosie? Sweezey	10
May 15 1881	J R Lightfoot-- Cora Powell	10
May 29 1881	William B Smith--Margarett A Brown	92
Aug 12, 1881	Herman Tollison--Jane Kidd	81

[Wit   Samuel C Brink & Mollie Edmonds   ]

Ministers and Justices who performed marriages Book " B "

1	Lewis D H Abrams, MG	37 A H Eaton, JP
2	David Adams, MG	38 C B Edgar, MG
3	John R Adams, MG	39 John F T Edwards,Pro J
4	Zenas Adams MG	40 J W. Finley, MG
5	J W Allcorn, JP	41 Herman Flachsbart, MG
6	Daniel Avers, --	42 Robert Fountaine,--
7	R S Banks, MG	43 C F Fortune, MG
8	T C Barrett MG	44 Wm L Gibson, MG
9	Samuel M Beard, MG	45 James Griffin, MG
10	M Bell MG	46 Benjamine Guyton, JP
11	John S Bell, JP	47 J W Handcock, JP
12	W E Bell JP	48 Samuel J Harkey, MG Mecs
13	John B Belmer, MG	49 George W Harlan Presby
14	J C Berryman, MG	50 J. S Harris, MG
15	Samuel Black, MG	51. John J Head, --
16	John R Boswell	52. John J Hennessay, C Pr
17	George Boulsher, MG	53 J R Hicks, MG MECS
18	H Bremer Evanc Luth	54 Sol R Hicks, MG MECS
19	B Brewington Presby	55 Joseph C Huff, JP
20	E W B Brewincton MG	56 J P Huff, MG
21	George F Brook, MG	57 W. G Huff, MG
22	H Brown MG	58, William Huff, MG Bapt
23	J R Burnham, MG	59 R M Jackson, MG
24	H Campbell MG	60 A M Jackson, MG
25	J M Carle, Bapt	61 Elijah Johnson Bapt
26	Gideon C Clark Presby	62 Jefferson Johnson, Bapt
27	Joel S Clark, MG	63 Nathan Johnson, JP
28	J T Clark --	64 Charles O. Jones MG
29	W H Cook, MG	65 John Kemper, JP
30	Wm H Copeland JP	66 J B Kinney, JP
31	William T Crocker, MG	67 Isaac Lane, MG
32	John Crowley, MG	68 T D Lewis MG
33	Franz Dinger, JP	69 H M Long, MG MECS
34.	John T. Donaldson Presby	70 Samuel Lucas, MG
35	I. H H Duff, MG Me	71 John S Luthy JP
36	John Duncan --	72 R K McCay Chap 3rd M C

73   B   S   McNail, MG
74   S   E   McNeely JP
75   D   J   Margins, MG
76   John Martin MG
77   Robert C Martin, Bapt
78   Mathew Martz. MG
79. Elias M Masters, MG
80   Fred A. Miller --
81   A   W   Milster, Mg, Presby
82   Alex S Moore. MG
83   Chas   S Obermeyer.
          St Paul, Farmington
84   Lewis Orrick, MG
85   George F Pierce --
86. A   J   Puls, JP
87. Chas   F   Quellmazl, MG
88   William Quesenberry, JP
89   Ira M Raney, JP
90. M   Reed, MG
91. Robert A Rich, MG
92   James M Ross, MG
93. Joel A Russell MG
94   Robert Seal, MG
95   James N Semonds JP
96   V. T   Settle, MG
97   W   T   Settle,--
98   Z   T   Settle, --
99   J   T   Shrum. Bapt
100 G   E   Shuler, JP
101 S   G   Shuler JP
102 R   N   Smith, MG
103 N   O   Sowers MG
104 Benj Steele MG
          Colored Church
105 Joseph L Stephens,--
106 Henry Thomas, MG
107 John Thomas, MG
108 W   H   Thompson
109 J   W   Tinley, MG
110 H Wallace Todd Presby
111 Magnes Tullock. Bapt
112 James H Vail C Judge
113 F   Walker, JP
114 Andrew Wallis MG
115 W   M   Wann? MG
116 Francis M Warren MG
117 J   J   Watts, MG MECS
118 John Webb MG
119 L   C   Werner, MG
120 L   W   Whitney JP
121 R   C   Williams. MG
122. John W Wood MG
123 H   J   Wray, MG
124 A   W   Wright MG

Iron County, Missouri Marriages
Book B 1873-1881

Index Book B

Abernathy 61
Abrams 76
Acres 67
Adell 71
Adams 59 62,68,69,76
Agien 64
Ahrens 59,60
Ake 63
Aker 56 59
Albert 58
Algeyer 63
Allcorn 63,76
Allen 54 62,65,71
Alleve 71
Allgier 71
Allison 60,71
Anderson 54,61,70
Angle 60
Anthony 76
Arisman 55
Arms 67
Armstrong 59,67
Arnett 64
Arnold 61,66
Arnoldi 75
Arnway 74
Asher 58
Aubersmith 68
Aubuchon 55 71
Audelein 57
Austin 60
Ayers 58 76
 B
Babcock 56 75
Baden 75
Bailey 54,64
Baird 69
Baier 75
Baker 60 62 71
Bales 60
Ballard 60
Banks 76
Barnes 58 68
Barrett 76
Barton 60
Base 58
Baumgardner 71
Baxter 60 61
Bay 56
Beacon 58
Beard 60 76
Bears 59

Bearsher 70
Beavers 62
Bebee 73,75
Beeman 68
Beck 58
Beel 57
Beers 59
Behm 64
Behrens 59,60
Belcher 66,72
Bell 55,56,67,69,74,76
Bellis 56,58,64
Bellor 65
Belmar 65,76
Bennett 58,64
Berryman 69,70,76
Bettis 55
Beucheman 61
Bird 57
Black 73,76
Blantonship 70
Block 73
Bodine 71
Boerttle 57
Bohms 74
Boles 66
Bollinger 59,61 73 74
Bond 54
Bone 61 68 71
Boon 64
Boss 58
Boswell 76
Boughen 57
Boulsher 76
Bounds 75
Bowls 64,66
Boyd 62
Bradey 70
Bradshaw 61,64
Branda 62
Breitenstein 64,76
Breman 74
Bremer 76
Bremington 76
Brent 69
Breslin 71
Breucer 56
Brewer 60 63 67
Brewington 66 72
Bridgewater 56
Brickey 57
Brink 76

Iron County, Missouri Marriages
Book B 1873-1881

Brooks 69 74,75,76
Brown 59 63,68 76
Bryan 69,72,75
Buckner 60,63,66.67 69,70
Buford 61,68
Bunnell 73
Burgan 55
Burgsmueller 75
Burk 72
Burke 61
Burks 59
Burnham 76
Burns 74
Bursheer 72
Burton 55
Buxton 65
Byrs 58
C
    Cagel 64
    Caldwell 54
    Campbell 54,55,56,61,66,68,72,
    74,75,76
    Canada 54,62
    Canning 64
    Carey 70
    Carle 76
    Carter 70,72 73
    Casey 61,66
    Casteel 68,72,73
    Chandion 68
    Chandler 54,55 59
    Chapman 63 66,72
    Charleton 63
    Chilton 63
    Chitty 58
    Church 74
    Christopher 58
    Clark 57 61,63,71,72,74,76
    Clayton 59
    Clements 54,55
    Clifton 60 68 70
    Clinton 75
    Cloud 55
    Clubb 66
    Coble 65 72
    Code 73
    Cogan 71
    Cole 66
    Coleman 74
    Collins 57,61,63,64,72
    Colt 73
    Conner 56
    Connell 72
    Conor 60

Conway 63
Cook 76
Cooley 64
Cooper 56,69,71
Copeland 69,76
Corbion 71
Cotter 60
Cotton 54,70
Counts 73
Cowan 67
Cox 60,62,65
Crawley 54
Creel 69
Crew 62
Crocker 54,59,60,62,63,65,
73,75,76
Cromstalk 72
    Cronkelton 56
    Crossland 62
    Cummel 55
    Cummingham 64
    Cummings 71
    Curtis 64,65
    Cuthbert 63
    D
Dace 57
Davidson 59
Davis 55,60,62,71,73
Davison 54,60
Dearing 54
Deboard 72
Delaney 75
Delano 54,57
Delashmit 75
Dellinger 55
Denison 60
Dennis 65
Demis 65
Denwiddy 56
Dequire 67
Deubo 62
DeWitt 59,69
Dewke 74
Deye 74
Dinger 56 57 76
Doll 70
Donaldson 76
Douglas 55
Doty 56
Dreyer 61
Dubs 56
Duff 76
Duncan 61,63
Dunn 59,66,71

Dunnegan 70
Dupri 65
    E
Earls 62
Eaton 76
Edgar 54,70,72,76
Edison 63
Edmonds 57,64,67,76
Edwards 59 61,62,76
Effinger 58
Eger 58
Eldridge 54,66
Elgin 70
Ellis 59
Erbe 72
Estes 54
Evans 65,66,67,70,75

    F
Falkner 62,64
Farley 68
Farr 63
Farrar 55
Fears 58
Ferguson 66
Ficht 75
Figart 59
Finley 73 76
Finton 64
Fisher 56 57,59 67,73
Fitzgibbens 71
Fitzpatrick 63 67
Flacsbart 76h
Fleischer 57
Fletcher 60 65
Flowers 73
Foguaide 70
Fokis 67
Forster 59
Fortune 76
Foster 72,74
Fountaine 76
Freeland 58
Fritzwater 74
Fuel 58
Fulcher 71
Fuller 59
    G
Game 62
Gankie 55
Ganter 61
Garrett 75
Gaston 72
Gehse 61

George 60 63
Gibson 64,76
Gilliam 69
Gilmore 64
Gilmn 61
Gleason 63
Goforth 56
Goggin 74
Goins 65
Good 70
Goodman 55,61,62
Gooman 72
Goverow 73
Gowen 54,67
Graham 54,63,64,66,70,73,
75
Gratiot 71
Grandhomme 57,72
Gray 65
Greason 65
Greenwood 65
Gregory 71
Griffin 76
Grims 65
Griffith 69
Guse 72,75
Guyfon 76
    H
Hale 56,57,58 60,66
Hall 54,55,63,75
Haller 57
Hamilton 68
Hammer 72
Hampton 62,67
Hancock 55 73 76
Hanlen 61
Harbison 60 67 68 69
Hardridge 55
Harkey 76
Harland 76
Harris 59 69,76
Harrison 54,57
Harrol 63
Hart 59
Hartridge 55
Harty 68
Harvey 70
Harviell 65,72
Hasting 59
Hauk 57
Hawk 73
Hawkins 55,58 59 60 63,64
Hay 59
Hayden 64

Hayward 72
Geisler 59
Head 76
Heaston 71,73
Heckman 60
Hedric 55,59
Hedsketh 70
Heinrich 57
Heitkamp 55
Henderson 60,63,68
Hendrich 62,65,71
Hennessay 76
Henson 55,57,67 69,73 75
Hess 63
Hickman 66,73
Hicks 76
Highley 57
Hilderbrand 60
Hill 58,66,67,70,74,75
Hillomen 75
Henson 66
Hockman 71
Hodge 75
Hofmeister 58
Hofner 63
Holland 68
Holloway 70
Holon 70
Holt 70
Hook 65
Hoinsey 65
Horton 62,70
House 65
Howe 61
Hubble 72
Huck 54
Huff 54 57 62,64,66,70,71,74 76
Huftmuster 60
Hugh 74
Hughes 55,56,61 64
Hyde 72 74
I
Inman 62,73,75
Irvin 55 66
J
Jackson 62,75,76
James 74
Jamison 70,73,75
Jauke 63
Jaycox 61
Jennings 69
Johle 68
Johnson 57 56 58 61 62 66 70 71
Joines 54   73 76

Jones 54,55,56,70 76
Joos 76
Jordon 58
Joyce 74
Justice 62,64
Kaiser 58,61
Kamhoby 75
Kanoholz 61
Kaufman 74
Keach 67
Keatherly 64
Keenan 76
Keel 75
Kellerman 75
Kelly 61,66,67,68
Kemper 69,76
Kennedy 56
Kerterson 62
Kesling 62
Ketting 58
Kessler 57
Ketcherside 67,68
Key 59,66
Kidd 76
Kimes 71
King 54,63,64,75
Kinney 76
Kipp 57
Kirchner 70
Kline 57
Knapp 71
Knees 67
Knight 54 66
Kocher 57
Kohn 58
Kolb 57
Kooth 56
Krumboltz 57
Krumph 68
L
Lamburt 70
Lamstedt 56
Langegger 76
Lane 58,76
Lashley 56 70
Lawson 71
Lax 56,68
Layman 57
Leage 69
Lear 60
Lee 56 65 69 73
Legget 61
Lemen 66
Lester 69

Levey 66
Lewis 60,61,62,65,68,70,73 75,76
Lick 54
Lindsey 56
Lightfoot 76
Lingham 65
Lloyd 68
Logan 56,63 68,73,74
Lomas 65
London 66
Long 59 76
Loomis 67
Louis 69
Love 67,75
Lovens 66
Lotz 63,67,68,71,73
Low 56
Lowe 67
Lowry 72 71
Loyd 61,73
Lucas 67,70
Lucy 72
Lufry 72
Luthon 71
Luthy 70
Luttrell 54
Lynch 74
     M
Mabee 55
Mac 58
Maise 75
Mann 73
Mannis 57
March 57
Marchbanks 65
Marquis 77
Markwell 65
Marlin 65
Marshall 76
Marlow 56
Marsters 56
Martin 55 56 57 58 59 60 63,65
Martz 77   67 77
Mase 75
Mason 56
Masters 77
Mathes 55 61
Matkins 68 73
May 56
Maybel 69
Mayberry 72
Maybury 67
Mayfeel 66
Mayor 72

Mayes 71,75
Mayfield 61,69
Mayhugh 61
Mays 59
McCalister 68
McCall 64
McCay 76
McClang 61
McClary 58
McCollough 70
McCue 66
McDonald 70
McFaddin 65
McGuire 73
McHenniss 65
McKenzie 59
McKinney 56,75
McMurty 68
McNail 77
McNeely 62,77
McQuire 64
McTadden 64
Mead 61,64
Mean 74
Meddus 64
Medley 60
Meeks 64
Merrill 54
Merrit 65 71
Messer 62
Meyer 58
Michel 55
Miller 54 57 58,60 63,68,
69,73,74
Milster 77
Minor 61
Mitchell 71
Moore 58,59,69,70,77
Monroe 62
Montgomery 58
Morgan 54
Morez 56
Morris 57,69
Morrison 62 67
Moses 69
Moss 69
Moyer 69
Muller 67
Mund 58
Mundy 73
Murphy 62 74
Murry 61
Musson 73
Myers 62 71,72 73

N
Nall 68
Nance 61 67,72
Neal 57
Needner 57
Neely 55,63
Nelson 59.62,73
Neuberger 54
Newman 58.61
Newton 58
Nichols 66
Nicholson 62
Nines 68
Norris 56,61,75
O
Oaks 75
O'Bannon 72
Obermeyer 77
Oesh 70
O'Leary 74
Oliver 75
Omohondro 66.72
Oneal 66.68
Orr 70
Orrick 77
Otridge 54
Owen 73
P
Packard 61
Palmer 72
Palymale 72
Panebecker 66
Pape 57
Parisco 64
Parker 65
Partese 55
Patrick 54
Patton 62
Payne 73
Peas 59
Peck 65
Peetz 72
Pemond 74
Pendergraft 56
Peterson 56
Petty 54
Pettyjohn 69
Philepa 73
Philips 55 56,58,60
Pierce 77
Pinder 57
Pinkley 57 63 67 71 74
Pormer 72
Potter 56

Powell 59,63,76
Pratt 59,69
Preslin 55
Preston 63
Price 56
Proffit 60,67
Prow 62
Puls 77
Q
Quellmazl 77
Quesenberry 54,77
R
Rahm 57
Randolph 68
Raney 54,68,72
Rapp 69
Raser 68
Ratlif 61
Rauft 75
Razor 64,68,71
Rease 54
Redding 63 64
Reece 57
Reed 61 62 63 65,66,69,
71 77
Reel 69
Reeves 54 64 66 74
Reimling 75
Revelle 67
Reyburn 73 75
Reynolds 60
Rhoades 61
Rich 77
Richey 56
Richter 57 58
Ringo 60
Rivers 73
Roan 72
Robbs 60 71
Roberson 58 75
Roberts 54
Rogers 56
Rolf 37
Rooker 55
Rose 70
Ross 77
Roth 65
Rouse 64 74
Rubel 69
Ruble 54 65 66 67
Rudy 71
Ruhl 68 70
Russell 56 58 59,64,66,67
68 69 72 73 77

Rust 71
Rutledge 65
Rutsman 58
  S
Sallee 55
Sanner 68
Scallon 73
Schaaf 57
Schaefer 75
Schaper 57
Schneider 56
Scheons 57
Schlieter 71
Schlueter 57,64,67
Schmidt 55,57,58,63,74
Schmidz 71
Schneider 72
Schwaner 58,74
Schubert 72
Schultz 71
Schutchfield 61
Seaford 56
Seal 68,77
Seals 69,70
Self 54
Selkirk 73
Sellar 65
Semands 68 77
Sequist 57
Settle 77
Shafer 59
Sharp 75
Shaver 57,68
Sheets 54
Shelton 72
Shepard 58,70
Sherill 62,63 66
Short 54,55
Shreave 72
Shrum 69 72,74,77
Shultz 75
Simmonds 59
Simmons 56,62 71
Simms 74
Simpson 54
Sing 65
Singleton 64
Sisco 57
Sizemore 62 67
Skimmerhun 56
Smith 54 55 57,59,60 62,63,64
65 69 70,72,74 76,77
Snead 60
Snodgrass 67

Sowers 77
Spencer 61,67
Spragley 70
Stagner 69
Stanalania 58
Stanton 58
StClair 69
Steadham 62
Steele 77
Steevens 68
Stemme 69
Stephens 60,77
Stepheson 60,64,66
Sternel 61
Stevens 56
Stevenson 61,64,68
Steward 74
Stewart 54
Stone 71
Stout 61,64
Stricklin 73
Studham 62
Sullivan 57,62,74
Sumpter 70
Sutherlin 57
[Southerland]
Sutterfield 64
Sutton 55,59,60 62,63,65,
67 69,70 73,74,75
Swanegan 66
Sweeney 76
Swiney 69
  T
Taber 61
Taul 64
Terrill 63 68
Tesrow 70
Tetwiler 56
Thomason 68
Thomas 55,59,63,69 71 77
Thorni 75
Thompson 57,58 63 66 67,
70,73 77
Tims 57
Tindel 60 61
Tinley 77
Todd 77
Tomaison 57
Tomlinson 69 76
Tong 55
Townson 55
Tranernicht 73
Tredway 65 75
Trollinger 69

Tulleck [a] 60 64,70,77
Turner 58 68,69
Turngate 56
Twitty 58
  U
Usrey 55
  V
Vail 77
Vancurran 66
Vandyke 58
Vance 74
Vandegrif 65,70
Vandergriss 57
Valle 63
Vaughn 74
Vest 62
Viesterson 59
Vineyard 74
  W
Wadle 66
Wadlow 66
Walker 77
Wallace 74
Wallas 60
Walles 70
Wallis 54,57,58 64,73,77
Walon 72
Walp 64
Walters 55,71
Wamack 71
Warren 54,56,60,64,67 77
Watts 77
Wauk 57
Weast 69
Webb 54,77
Weise 59
Weiss 56
Welch 58 69
Welmer 77
Werner 77
Wesley 69
West 65
Westbrook 57
Westerman 69
White 57 61
Whitney 77
Whitsett 63
Whitworth 72
Wiatt 59,75
Wickman 58
Wiett 69
Wilbank 62
Wiley 74
Will 68

Willbite 59,65
William 59,60,65,66,67,68
72,74,77
Wilson 57,58,65,66
Winengar 60
Winfield 54
Wiseman 57,60
Wolf 67,71
Womack 57
Woods 59 62,63,66,77
Worille 74
Workhouser 74
Worton 65
Wray 77
Wren 56
Wright 77
Wyatt 55,67
  Y
Yarbaugh 65
Yates 68
Young 61
  Z
Zude 55 68

Portions of Book C Iron Co Mo
Iron Co Newspapers

July 11 1882   Cyrus B Miner --Sarah Jane Strickland

Dec 7, 1882   James Henry Dennis--Rosa E Keith

Dec 21 1882   Joshua Midgett--Martha E Miller

May 9, 1883   Huston Latham --Anna Bell

June 11 1883   Jesse Hedgecoth Jr --Ady Bell

July 30, 1883   William B Brooks--Ida F Hauk

Sept 4, 1883   George W Brooks--Mary Hawk

Oct 6, 1883   Marian Newman--Julia Bell

Nov 30, 1883   James M Smith--Martha A. Love

Mar 6, 1884   James Crownover--Amanda Ratliff

June 20, 1884   James T Davis--June Webb

Aug 25, 1884   Levi F Crownover--Lissey Allen

Oct 30 1884   Joseph Webb--Jennie [Graves] Grimes

May 19, 1887   Wyatt King--Elizabeth Pryor

July 7 1887   James W Webb--Vasa E Jones

July 16, 1887   Huston Latham--Martha J Newman

Aug 25, 1887   Jordon E Robinette--Nancy E Stevens

Oct 10, 1887   John Harbison--Louise Rebor[er]

Dec 6, 1887   Henry Damonian?--Lucy Webb

Nov 24, 1887   Samuel F Wigger--Mary Mann

Dec 7, 1887   Lavender Eamonds--Julia Carty

Aug 25, 1888   Alexander Smith--Susan Crownover

Oct 13 1888   Monroe D Carty--Clara Belcher

Dec 22 1888   William Fakes--Rebecca L Crownover

Feb 1 1889   William D Troutman--Eliza F Brooks

Dec 1 1884   Nelson Adams Sr --Mrs Manerva Henson

Jan 13, 1885   Jesse Copeland--Mary E Sumpter

Portions of Book C Iron Co   Mo
Iron Co   Newspapers

Jan   30, 1885   Lafayette Alcorn--Alice Love

Feb   14, 1885   Paschal Buford--Sarah A Middleton

Nov. 7, 1885   Henry Stricklin--Martha Shrum

Mar   4, 1886   Samuel T Dennison--Anna Bois

Mar   8, 1886   Henry Sumpter--Mary Susan Clemons

Oct   8, 1886   John Q. Adams--Eliza A Stevenson

Feb   19, 1887 George W. Cain--Ella J Highley
These marriages listed above do not include all the marriages
in book "C" only those marriages that I had in my notes for
use in research I nave done in the past. The next marriages
are taken from newspapers that have published a death and
included their marriage I have only taken down name of which
I have some knowledge and many marriages were not recorded by
me Almost all these families spent some are all of their
life in Iron County Some of these marriages may be recorded
in Iron County, Madison County, Washington County or St.
Francois marriages at the court house I never made any
attempt to verify this in most cases

Newspaper Death Notice

June 12, 1875 Joseph Black--Jane Williams

Sept 29 1842 John W Cooley--E A Sherill

Jan   29, 1827 I S Harvey--Sarah Jane------

April   1865 E R Haywood--Sarah F Stevens

July 5, 1881   James B Maxwell--Lucy A. Carty

Sept 1 1831 William Wilkerson--Caroline Collins

Feb   16, 1882 E R Haywood- -Lizzie Campbell

Sept 21 1856 Jerry Green--Judith P ------

Jan   15 1857 J E Low--Margaret M ------

May 29 1851   Valentine Hughes-- Edmond Hicks

Nov 15 1852 George Bush--Sarah Singleton

July 15, 1852 George Cain--Sally Langly

May 10 1853   John Cartee--Polly Gridei

Sept 22 1853 James George--Martha Carty

Jan   22 1854   Charles L Edmonds--Jane Copeland

Oct   30, 1854 Samuel Hilderbrand--Margaret Hampton
Sam Hilderbrand is the noted bushwacker during the Civil War
and Margaret is the granddaughter of Henry Fry.

Feb   22, 1855 William H Copeland--Mary A McNail

Mar   5, 1857   James Dobbins-- Amy Cartee [Carty]

April 21 1857 James Murry--Mary Jane Cartee

Dec   16, 1857 Alfred Rudy--Elizabeth Cantrell

Nov   25. 1858 Washington Hilderbrand--Polly Eastes

          1833   Joseph Bollinger--Elizabeth White

          1832   Rev John Thomas--Anne McMurtey

Nov   17, 1872 T Jefferson Hampton--Emaline--------

Feb   21. 1854 Joseph M. Ringo--Fredonia A McGregor

Dec   27, 1887 Harvey Drewry--Nannie Bell

Nov   15. 1838 Moses P Collins--M Elmira Wilson

          1826   Tobins Dinger-- Christina--------

July 19. 1888 Augustus Orrick--Miss Wilson

          1840   Rev J C Williams--Susan F -------

Mar   24. 1836 Joseph L. Stephens--Louiza W Wyatt

Feb   7, 1887   J A Middleton--Laura E. Jane Vaughn

Jan   27, 1852 Charles H Westerman-- Elizabeth Harbison

Jan   28. 1867 James Buford--Marie Louisa Bacon

          1850   W Adolphus Welch--Henrietta Kunkelman

Apr   17, 1890 Flem Kidd--Mary Lathan

          1864   Mr Towl--Ann Kendall

June 17, 1858 Edward Latham--Angeline Hillon

Mar   14 1842 John R McKinney--Martha Johnson

Sept 4. 1890   William Carty--Martha Belcher

Portions of Book C Iron Co Mo
Iron Co Newspapers

July   1841   John Webb--Susan Bridgewater

Nov 25, 1852   William E Fitzpatrick--Precilla Carty

May 25, 1880   John A. Hogue--Mollie Howell

            1832   John V Logan--Elizabeth H Mallow

            1822   Mr Thompson--Diana Howard

Oct 19, 1892   Albert Nipper--Josephine Webb

            1830   John Sutton--Elizabeth-------

Mar 18, 1891   John B Hodge--Theodosia E. Scoggins

Dec 15, 1864   William H. Bonney--Eliza Ranft

Nov. 23, 1853   Issac M Thomas--Susan J Johnson

Dec. 14, 1894   John F Keith--M Anderson

Mar 26 1835   Frederick Woolford--Eliza J Logan

Dec 23, 1875   Francis J Henderson--Mary E Logan

Oct 17 1894   Rev J H Turner--Rose Hartman

            1852   Westley Sherrell--Martha Alcorn

Dec 2 1892   Leanord Richardson- Cora Harral

Feb 11, 1891   Monroe Black -Mollie Johnston

Mar 11, 1856   Andrew J Carty--Elvira Love

Dec.   1852   William Wyatt--Marie Imbiden

Sept 24, 1859 Mathew Bartlow--Lucy Ann Fitzpatrick

Apr 10 1866   Rev A W wright--Mary J Mann

Oct 26, 1837   William R Moyer--Susan Rice

Aug 27 1857   John G Imboden--Mary E Petty

Feb. 16, 1843   James W Stephens--Emeline------

Oct 14 1945   James T Cox--Caroline M Edwards

Fall of 1850   Anthoney Koeth--Mary Ann Cook

Jan 21 1869   W R Patterson--Sarah A Cincannon

Portions of Book C Iron Co Mo
Iron Co Newspapers

Mar   14 1894   S A Reyburn--Mrs S Alexander[Nee Robison]

        1855   Jonathan Richardson--Nancy--------
Catherine Reyburn 1st m Jonas Henderson 2nd m George D Sloan
Jan   13, 1863

May 12, 1899   Norman White--Nora Wilson

        1848   R M Omobundro--Matilda F Clarkson

April   1889   Milton Maughlin--Lena Kolwitch

March   1862   Judge William Carter--Marie McElvaine

Sept 18 1849 William Thomas--Carrie R Digges

Jan 8, 1868   Walker Brown--Sarah J Doty

Mar 6, 1887   Franklin Sutton--Mary Payne

Elder James C Williams 1st marriage Lydia Waller, 2nd Nancy
Jefferies 1856   William died in 1861 Believed to be the
well known minister and brother of Peter Williams who founded
the Salem Church near Redmondville in the late 1820's

Sept 18, 1884 William P Hall--Eva Ligget

Aug 13 1857 William Imboden--Margaret Shelton

Judge Warren C Johnson--1st Elizabeth J Stone Nov 1850,
2nd Susan J Thomas Nov 1862

Sept 18, 1890   J B Jennings -Maggie Latham

        1872   James H Clark--Mary J Whitworth

        1881   Nugent Kidd--Mary Roop

        1855   Benjamine Kidd--Mary Thomas

        1865   B C Fitts--Missouri Hodges

Jan 24 1867 John D Stephens--Patsy Imboden

Nov 10 1853 Cyrus Russell--Delia Clark

May 25 1863   Thomas Newman--Jane Carter May

Nov 6, 1876   Monroe Fitzpatrick--Frankie M Edmonds

Dec 20 1860 William H Buford--Iowa Gullivar

Nov 24, 1892 R L Daniel--Gracie A Tant

Portions of Book C Iron Co Mo
Iron Co Newspapers

      1853   John J W Miller--Rebecca R Sutton

July 30, 1851   Robert Lewis--Mary Griffith

Jan 29. 1852   Matthew Adams--Josephine Gallaher

Mar 30, 1887   Walter L Latham--Isabel Imboden

Mar 4, 1858   P C Carty--Lander Black

     1867   Andy Lewis--Angeline Jackson

Sept 15, 1865   Jasper Brummet--Lucinda Litteral

Joseph Hasty 1st m Malinda Galtney 2nd m Catherine Shrum Mar. 5, 1858

Jan 14, 1859   Jasper Orrick--Elizabeth Edmonds

Apr 20, 1870   Alfred Hale--Annie Elizabeth Padfield

Feb   1869   James A George--Helen Miller

Oct. 26, 1876   George Sherrill--Mary Jane Pinkley